Human Behavior in the Macro Social Environment

FOURTH EDITION

Karen Kirst-Ashman
University of Wisconsin, Whitewater

Prepared by

Vicki Vogel
University of Wisconsin, Whitewater

BROOKS/COLE
CENGAGE Learning·

Australia • Brazil • Japan • Korea • Mexico • Singapore • Spain • United Kingdom • United States

For product information and technology assistance, contact us at **Cengage Learning Customer & Sales Support, 1-800-354-9706**

For permission to use material from this text or product, submit all requests online at **www.cengage.com/permissions** Further permissions questions can be emailed to **permissionrequest@cengage.com**

ISBN-13: 978-1-285-41867-4
ISBN-10: 1-285-41867-0

Brooks/Cole
20 Davis Drive
Belmont, CA 94002-3098
USA

Cengage Learning is a leading provider of customized learning solutions with office locations around the globe, including Singapore, the United Kingdom, Australia, Mexico, Brazil, and Japan. Locate your local office at: **www.cengage.com/global**

Cengage Learning products are represented in Canada by Nelson Education, Ltd.

To learn more about Brooks/Cole, visit **www.cengage.com/brookscole**

Purchase any of our products at your local college store or at our preferred online store **www.cengagebrain.com**

Printed in the United States of America
1 2 3 4 5   17 16 15 14 13

Contents

NOTE TO INSTRUCTORS:
The exercises that appear in this workbook are also in the Instructor's Resource Manual including Commentary to Instructors sections for each exercise that provide information and/or answers for the exercises.

Empowerment Series

Dear Social Work Student,

Welcome to the *Competencies/Practice Behaviors Workbook* for Kirst-Ashman's *Human Behavior in the Macro Social Environment*, 4e. Throughout your course you will acquire a great deal of new knowledge, including an introduction to new theories, informative research, and practical skills like critical thinking skills and frameworks for appreciating and overcoming challenges. All of the knowledge you gain will offer you a deeper, richer understanding of social work. Used in conjunction with your text and other resources, the *Competencies/Practice Behaviors Workbook* presents you with Practice Exercises that will teach you how to transform your new knowledge into social work Practice Behaviors.

About Competence and Practice Behaviors

In social work, the words Competence and Practice Behavior have a unique meaning beyond the typical dictionary definitions. "Competence" in the usual sense means that a person possesses suitable skills and abilities to do a specific task. A competent baseball player must move quickly, catch, throw, and play as part of a team. They also have to think quickly, understand the rules of the game, and be knowledgeable of their environment. In the same way, a competent social worker should be able to do a number of job-related duties, think critically, and understand the context of their work. The Council on Social Work Education (CSWE) has defined specific Core Competency areas for all social work students, and their corresponding Practice Behaviors as follows:

Competencies and Practice Behaviors
2.1.1: Identify as a Professional Social Worker and Conduct Oneself Accordingly
a. Advocate for client access to the services of social work
b. Practice personal reflection and self-correction to assure continual professional development
c. Attend to professional roles and boundaries
d. Demonstrate professional demeanor in behavior, appearance, and communication
e. Engage in career-long learning
f. Use supervision and consultation
2.1.2: Apply Social Work Ethical Principles to Guide Professional Practice
a. Recognize and manage personal values in a way that allows professional values to guide practice
b. Make ethical decisions by applying standards of the National Association of Social Workers Code of Ethics and, as applicable, of the International Federation of Social Workers/ International Association of Schools of Social Work Ethics in Social Work, Statement of Principles
c. Tolerate ambiguity in resolving ethical conflicts
d. Apply strategies of ethical reasoning to arrive at principled decisions

2.1.3: Apply Critical Thinking to Inform and Communicate Professional Judgments	
a.	Distinguish, appraise, and integrate multiple sources of knowledge, including research-based knowledge and practice wisdom
b.	Analyze models of assessment, prevention, intervention, and evaluation
c.	Demonstrate effective oral and written communication in working with individuals, families, groups, organizations, communities, and colleagues
2.1.4: Engage Diversity and Difference in Practice	
a.	Recognize the extent to which a culture's structures and values may oppress, marginalize, alienate, or create or enhance privilege and power
b.	Gain sufficient self-awareness to eliminate the influence of personal biases and values in working with diverse groups
c.	Recognize and communicate their understanding of the importance of difference in shaping life experiences
d.	View themselves as learners and engage those with whom they work as informants
2.1.5: Advance Human Rights and Social and Economic Justice	
a.	Understand the forms and mechanisms of oppression and discrimination
b.	Advocate for human rights and social and economic justice
c.	Engage in practices that advance social and economic justice
2.1.6: Engage in Research-Informed Practice and Practice-Informed Research	
a.	Use practice experience to inform scientific inquiry
b.	Use research evidence to inform practice
2.1.7: Apply Knowledge of Human Behavior and the Social Environment	
a.	Utilize conceptual frameworks to guide the processes of assessment, intervention, and evaluation
b.	Critique and apply knowledge to understand person and environment
2.1.8: Engage in Policy Practice to Advance Social and Economic Well-Being and to Deliver Effective Social Work Services	
a.	Analyze, formulate, and advocate for policies that advance social well-being
b.	Collaborate with colleagues and clients for effective policy action
2.1.9: Respond to Contexts that Shape Practice	
a.	Continuously discover, appraise, and attend to changing locales, populations, scientific and technological developments, and emerging societal trends to provide relevant services
b.	Provide leadership in promoting sustainable changes in service delivery and practice to improve the quality of social services
2.1.10: Engage, Assess, Intervene, and Evaluate with Individuals, Families, Groups, Organizations and Communities	
a.	Substantively and affectively prepare for action with individuals, families, groups, organizations, and communities
b.	Use empathy and other interpersonal skills
c.	Develop a mutually agreed-on focus of work and desired outcomes
d.	Collect, organize, and interpret client data
e.	Assess client strengths and limitations
f.	Develop mutually agreed-on intervention goals and objectives
g.	Select appropriate intervention strategies
h.	Initiate actions to achieve organizational goals
i.	Implement prevention interventions that enhance client capacities
j.	Help clients resolve problems

k.	Negotiate, mediate, and advocate for clients
l.	Facilitate transitions and endings
m.	Critically analyze, monitor, and evaluate interventions

Each of the Exercises in the *Competencies/Practice Behaviors Workbook* will focus on learning and applying social work Practice Behaviors. While every Exercise will not ask you to apply Competencies or Practice Behaviors from every Core Competency area, by the time you finish your course you will have practiced many and gained a better working knowledge of how social work is done. The goal, shared by your professors, your program, the authors of this text, and by Brooks/Cole, Cengage Learning Social Work team, is that by the end of your curriculum you will have honed your Practice Behaviors in all of the Core Competency areas into a skill set that empowers you to work effectively as a professional social worker.

Assessing Competence: Partnering with Your Instructor and Peer Evaluator
As described above, the Council on Social Work Education clearly defines the Competencies and Practice Behaviors that a social work student should be trained to employ. Therefore, the grading rubric that comes at the end of every chapter of the *Competencies/Practice Behaviors Workbook* is adapted from Competencies and Practice Behaviors defined by CSWE (see the table above). To assess your competence during your course, we recommend you partner with a peer(s) who can act as your course "evaluator(s)" to genuinely assess both your written assignments and your role-plays; be sure to ask your professor to comment on and approve the assessments once they are completed by you and your Evaluator. It is our hope that partnering with your classmates in this way will familiarize you with the unique learning opportunity you will have in your Field Experience – the signature pedagogy of social work education. There you will apply all of your knowledge and skills under the supervision of your Field Instructor and Field Liaison before completing your required curriculum.

As always, we thank you for your commitment to education and to the profession. Enjoy your course, and *feel empowered to help others*!

Chapter 1
Introduction to Human Behavior in the Macro Social Environment

Competencies/Practice Behaviors Exercise 1.1
Where Do You Come From?

Focus Competencies or Practice Behaviors:

- EP 2.1.1b   Practice personal reflection and self-correction to assure continual professional development
- EP 2.1.4c   Recognize and communicate their understanding of the importance of difference in shaping life experiences
- EP 2.1.10a   Substantively and affectively prepare for action with individuals, families, groups, organizations, and communities

A.   Brief Description

You describe your community of origin, compare these backgrounds with each other, and analyze community strengths and weaknesses.

B.   Objectives

You will:

1.   Describe the community where you grew up.
2.   Compare your own community of origin with others.
3.   Evaluate variables that contribute to the strengths or weaknesses of a community in order to understand the ways a community social system "promote[s] or deter[s] people in maintaining or achieving health and well-being."[1]

C.   Procedure

1.   Review the content on variables characterizing communities.
2.   Individually write down your answers to the questions posed below that focus on a range of variables (italicized below in section D) characterizing your home communities (Kirst-Ashman & Hull, 2009).
3.   Form small groups of four to six.
4.   Share your descriptions of your home communities with others in the group, and compare and contrast these descriptions. (A volunteer from each group should be prepared to share the group's findings with the entire class in a subsequent discussion.)
5.   After about 10 minutes, terminate your discussions and participate in a full-class discussion concerning your findings.

---

[1] See *EPAS* EP 2.1.7. ("Apply knowledge of human behavior and the social environment.")

6. A representative from each group will share her or his summary of the discussion. Comments from others are encouraged.

7. Discuss what aspects contribute to the strengths and weaknesses of a community. How would you describe an *ideal* community?

D. Instructions for Students

1. Write down answers to the following questions about the community in which you grew up.

    a. *Rural or urban setting.* Would you characterize your home community as being in the country, a small town, a medium-sized city, a major metropolis, or a suburb of a bigger city?

    b. *Population density.* How many people live in your community of origin? Would you describe the area as being spread out, crowded, or something between the two?

    c. *General standard of living.* How would you describe the social class of people living in the community? Poor? Middle-class? Fairly well-to-do? Wealthy?

    d. *Housing.* What are the residents' homes like? Do most residents own their own property, or do they rent houses or apartments? How would you describe the quality of the homes? Older? Newer? Run-down? Well-kept? Are dwellings bunched together and cramped, or do homes have spacious yards? Does adequate affordable housing exist to meet community residents' needs?

    e. *Available resources.* To what extent are hospitals, parks, police and fire protection, garbage collection, and shopping readily available? Are there services and resources accessible for people in need including shelters for battered women, crisis intervention hotlines, food pantries, counseling, and other social services?

    f. *Spiritual opportunities.* Are there churches and religious organizations in the community? How many? To what extent do community residents pursue spiritual involvement?

    g. *Education.* How would you characterize the educational system in your home community? Is it generally considered "good," "effective," "poor" or "substandard"? How does it compare with educational systems in neighboring communities? How would you describe the education you received there?

    h. *Other factors.* What other aspects of your home community are important to you and why?

    i. *Summary impression.* When you think of your home community, what words first come to mind? How would you describe it to a complete stranger? What would you emphasize? Was it a generally happy, pleasant place? Or was it hostile, dangerous, and impoverished? What are the reasons for your answers?

Competencies/Practice Behaviors Exercise 1.2
Comparing and Contrasting Theoretical Terms

Focus Competencies or Practice Behaviors:
- EP 2.1.3a   Distinguish, appraise, and integrate multiple sources of knowledge, including research-based knowledge and practice wisdom
- EP 2.1.7a   Utilize conceptual frameworks to guide the processes of assessment, intervention, and evaluation

A.   Brief Description

You will compare and contrast basic terms inherent in systems theories and the ecological approach.

B.   Objectives

You will:
1.   Recognize the basic terms in systems theories and the ecological perspective in order to "utilize [these] conceptual frameworks to guide the processes of assessment" and "intervention."[2]
2.   Examine the differences between terms in the two approaches.
3.   "Critique and apply knowledge [about these theories] to understand person and environment."[3]

C.   Procedure

1.   Review the material on systems theories and the ecological perspective including definitions of terms.
2.   Divide the class into small groups of four to six.
3.   The instructor will read the scenarios presented below one at a time to the class.
4.   Discuss the similarities and differences among the systems and ecological terms identified below. (Each group should select a representative who will be prepared to report to the entire class the small group's findings.)
5.   After 10 to 15 minutes, you will terminate your discussions and participate in a full-class discussion.
6.   A representative from each group will be asked to share her or his summary of the discussion. Comments from others in the class are encouraged.

D.   Instructions for Students

Read the similarities and differences among the terms in systems theories and the ecological perspective.

---

[2] See *EPAS* EP 2.1.7.
[3] See *EPAS* EP 2.1.7.

Systems Terms	Definition
System	A set of elements that are orderly, interrelated, and a functional whole.
Boundaries	Repeatedly occurring patterns that characterize the relationships within a system and give that system a particular identity.
Subsystem	A secondary or subordinate system within a larger system.
Homeostasis	The tendency for a system to maintain a relatively stable, constant state of balance.
Role	A culturally expected behavior pattern for a person having a specified status or being involved in a designated social relationship.
Relationship	The dynamic interpersonal connection between two or more persons or systems that involves how they think about, feel about, and behave toward each other.
Input	The energy, information, or communication flow received from other systems.
Output	What happens to input after it has gone through and been processed by some system.
Feedback	A special form of input where a system receives information about that system's own performance.
Negative feedback	Feedback where, as the result, a system can choose to correct any deviations or mistakes and return to a more homeostatic state.
Positive feedback	The informational input a system receives about what it is doing correctly in order to maintain itself and thrive.
Interface	The point where two systems (including individuals, families, groups, organizations, or communities) come into contact with each other, interact, or communicate.
Differentiation	A system's tendency to move from a simple to a more complex existence.
Entropy	The natural tendency of a system to progress toward disorganization, depletion, and death.
Negative entropy	The process of a system toward growth and development.
Equifinality	The fact that there are many different means to achieve the same end.

Ecological Terms	Definition
Social environment	The conditions, circumstances, and human interactions that encompass human beings.
Energy	The natural power of active involvement between people and their environment.
Input	A form of energy coming into a person's life and adding to that life.
Output	A form of energy going out of a person's life or taking something away from it.

4

Interface	The exact point where the interaction between an individual and the environment takes place.
Adaptation	The capacity to adjust to surrounding environmental conditions.
"Person-in-environment fit"	The extent to which "the needs, capacities, behavioral styles, and goals of people" fit or match "the characteristics of the environment" (Gitterman & Germain, 2008, p. 55).
Stressor	"A demand, situation, or circumstance" that results in physiological and/or emotional tension (i.e., stress) (Zastrow & Kirst-Ashman, 2013, p. 634).
Stress	The resulting physiological and/or emotional tension produced by a stressor that affects a person's internal balance.
Coping	A form of adaptation where people respond to stress by expending effort to change (1) their own behavioral, cognitive, or emotional reactions; (2) the environmental conditions contributing to the stress; (3) the interaction between their own reactions and the environment; or (4) some combination of these responses (Gitterman & Germain, 2008).
Relatedness	"The capacity to form attachments" (Payne, 2005, p. 151).
Habitat	"The physical and social settings of people" (Payne, 2005, p. 151).
Niche	"The particular social position held" by a person within the social structure of the habitat (Payne, 2005, p. 151).

Competencies/Practice Behaviors Exercise 1.3
Applying Theoretical Concepts to Macro Practice Situations

Focus Competencies or Practice Behaviors:
- EP 2.1.7a   Utilize conceptual frameworks to guide the processes of assessment, intervention, and evaluation
- EP 2.1.7b   Critique and apply knowledge to understand person and environment
- EP 2.1.10a   Substantively and affectively prepare for action with individuals, families, groups, organizations, and communities

A.   Brief Description

You will apply concepts inherent in systems theories to one case scenario and those basic to the ecological perspective to another scenario. Discussion of findings will follow.

B. **Objectives**
    You will:
    1. Apply theoretical concepts inherent in the conceptual frameworks of systems theories and the ecological perspective to case scenarios reflecting macro practice goals.
    2. "Critique and apply knowledge [about these theories] to understand person and environment."[4]

C. **Procedure**
    1. Review the material on systems theories and the ecological perspective including definitions of terms.
    2. The class will be divided into small groups of four to six.
    3. The instructor will read the scenarios presented below to the class one at a time.
    4. The groups will discuss the subsequent questions. (You should also select a group representative who will be prepared to report to the entire class the small groups' findings.)
    5. After about 10 minutes for each scenario's small group discussion, the small groups will terminate their discussions and participate in a full-class discussion.
    6. A representative from each group will be asked to share her or his summary of the discussion. Comments from others in class are encouraged.

D. **Instructions for Students**
    Read each of the following scenarios and respond to the subsequent questions. Relate concepts involved in systems theories or the ecological perspective as indicated.

> *Scenario #1:* A social worker employed by a neighborhood center determines that the range of workers and other professionals working with various adolescent clients within the community are not communicating with each other. For example, school social workers have no established procedure for conveying information to protective services workers who, in turn, do not communicate readily with probation and parole workers. This is despite the fact that most of these professionals are working with many of the same clients. The neighborhood center social worker decides to pull together representatives from the various involved agencies and establish more clearly defined communication channels.
>
> How can concepts inherent in systems theories be used to describe what's happening in this scenario? Identify which concepts apply and how. Concepts include: *system; boundaries; subsystem; homeostasis; roles; relationships; input; output; negative and positive feedback; interface; differentiation; entropy; negative entropy; and equifinality.*

---

[4] See *EPAS* EP 2.1.7.

> **Scenario #2:** A juvenile probation officer is distressed by a proposed legislative action to delete a vocational training program for juvenile offenders because of its expense. He talks to other workers and administrators in his state agency, and gathers facts and statistics that support the program's cost effectiveness. He then begins calling and writing involved legislators and sets up a meeting with the chairperson of the legislative committee that recommended the program's deletion. Additionally, he contacts other concerned social workers and encourages them to participate in similar activities.
>
> How can concepts inherent in the ecological perspective be used to describe what's happening in this scenario? Identify which concepts apply and how. Concepts include: *the social environment; energy; input; output; interface; adaptation; person-in-environment fit; stress, stressors, and coping; relatedness; habitat; niche; competence; self-esteem; and self-direction.*

Competencies/Practice Behaviors Exercise 1.4
Systems and Practice Scenarios in the Macro Social Environment

---

Focus Competencies or Practice Behaviors:
- EP 2.1.7a   Utilize conceptual frameworks to guide the processes of assessment, intervention, and evaluation
- EP 2.1.7b   Critique and apply knowledge to understand person and environment
- EP 2.1.10a Substantively and affectively prepare for action with individuals, families, groups, organizations, and communities

A.   Brief Description

You will be given a number of case scenarios involving macro practice goals. You will then determine and discuss the target of change, the micro systems, the mezzo systems, the macro systems, and the macro client system involved in each.

B.   Objectives

You will:

1.   Examine a range of scenarios involving macro practice goals pursued by direct service practitioners "to guide the processes of assessment" and "intervention."[5]

2.   Identify the target of change (involving micro, mezzo, and macro systems) and the macro client system involved in each with the intention of promoting people's achievement and maintenance of "health and well-being."[6]

3.   "Critique and apply knowledge [about targets of change and macro client systems] to understand person and environment."[7]

---

[5] See *EPAS* EP 2.1.7.
[6] See *EPAS* EP 2.1.7.
[7] See *EPAS* EP 2.1.7.

C. **Procedure**
   1. Review the material on systems including the concepts of target of change, micro system, mezzo system, macro system, client system, and macro client system.
   2. The instructor will read each of the following scenarios and ask the class to respond to the subsequent questions. Handouts of the scenarios and questions may be distributed as well.

D. **Instructions for Students**
   1. Read the following scenarios and respond to the following questions.

> ***Scenario A:*** A local charitable funding organization decides to cut off its funding contribution to a Planned Parenthood agency that has three satellite clinics in addition to its larger, centrally located main clinic. The result would be a severe cutback in services including the closure of at least two of its satellite clinics. A huge number of clients would find it difficult if not impossible to receive adequate services. A social work counselor at one of the clinics, with the support of her supervisor, gathers facts to support her argument that funding is necessary and arranges a meeting with the funding organization's leaders to discuss the cuts and try to persuade these leaders to change their minds.

What is the *target of change?*
What *micro systems* are involved?
What *mezzo systems* are involved?
What *macro systems* are involved?
What is the *macro client system?*

> ***Scenario B:*** A social worker employed by a large public social services department hears increasing numbers of complaints from clients about drug houses popping up in their residential neighborhoods. The worker identifies clients and other concerned citizens in the communities and organizes a community meeting. She then assists community residents in formulating a plan to band together, identify drug house locations, and establish a procedure to report such houses to the authorities.

What is the *target of change?*
What *micro systems* are involved?
What *mezzo systems* are involved?
What *macro systems* are involved?
What is the *macro client system?*

Scenario C: The main tasks of a Foster Care Unit is to assess potential foster parent applicants, monitor placement and manage cases as they move in and out of foster care, and train foster parents in parenting and behavior management skills. The unit social workers hold bi-weekly meetings where they discuss how to improve agency service provision. The workers take turns organizing the meetings and running the discussions.

What is the *target of change?*
What *micro systems* are involved?
What *mezzo systems* are involved?
What *macro systems* are involved?
What is the *macro client system?*

Scenario D: A social worker employed by a large private family services agency specializes in international adoptions, especially those involving Russia and China. He discovers that many of the adoptive children are experiencing health problems resulting from early nutritional deprivation. The worker feels that the problem goes beyond one or two cases, but reflects a serious pattern. No referral process is in place to automatically assess adoptive children and refer them to needed resources, including designated medical specialists. The worker begins to establish a systematic process for assessment and referral.

What is the *target of change?*
What *micro systems* are involved?
What *mezzo systems* are involved?
What *macro systems* are involved?
What is the *macro client system?*

Scenario E: Agency administration asks one of three social workers in a large residential health care complex for older adults to assess the effectiveness of its social services program.

What is the *target of change?*
What *micro systems* are involved?
What *mezzo systems* are involved?
What *macro systems* are involved?
What is the *macro client system?*

Scenario F: A social worker at a public assistance agency is terribly troubled by the conditions of the agency's waiting room for clients and by the tedious process required for clients' intakes. She explores the issue, develops a proposed plan for improvement, and makes an appointment to speak with the agency's executive director about it.

9

What is the *target of change?*
What *micro systems* are involved?
What *mezzo systems* are involved?
What *macro systems* are involved?
What is the *macro client system?*

Scenario G: A group of community residents approach a social worker about starting up a Neighborhood Watch program. (*Neighborhood Watch* programs involve neighborhood residents coming together and making a commitment to prevent crime in their neighborhood. They devise a system for observing any suspicious behavior, especially on the part of strangers, and for alerting the proper authorities in order to deter crime. Members also usually educate new people moving into the neighborhood about the program and publicize that the program exists via window decals and signs.) The worker provides community residents both with encouragement and some information about how to go about it.

What is the *target of change?*
What *micro systems* are involved?
What *mezzo systems* are involved?
What *macro systems* are involved?
What is the *macro client system?*

Competencies/Practice Behaviors Exercise 1.5
Using Critical Thinking Skills

Focus Competencies or Practice Behaviors:
- EP 2.1.2a   Recognize and manage personal values in a way that allows professional values to guide practice
- EP 2.1.3a   Distinguish, appraise, and integrate multiple sources of knowledge, including research-based knowledge and practice wisdom
- EP 2.1.4c   Recognize and communicate their understanding of the importance of difference in shaping life experiences
- EP 2.1.8a   Analyze, formulate, and advocate for policies that advance social well-being
- EP 2.1.9a   Continuously discover, appraise, and attend to changing locales, populations, scientific and technological developments, and emerging societal trends to provide relevant services

A.   Brief Description
You are asked to determine how you might assess some important issues in the macro social environment and use critical thinking skills.

B.   Objectives

You will:
1.   "Use critical thinking" to identify relevant questions to ask about a designated issue.[8]
2.   "Recognize and manage personal values" and opinions about controversial social issues, and your rationales for such opinions.[9]
3.   Evaluate your assumptions after viewing the issue from other perspectives to pave the way for allowing "professional values to guide practice."[10]
4.   Begin to "apply strategies of ethical reasoning to arrive at principled decisions."[11]

C.   Procedure
1.   Review the material on the critical thinking process using the Triple A approach:
Ask questions.
Assess the established facts and issues involved.
Assert a concluding opinion.
2.   The following questions will be presented one at a time:
a.   Should murderers receive the death penalty?
b.   In view of limited resources for health care, should children and young adults be given priority over older adults as recipients of expensive treatments (for example, transplanted organs or extensive cancer treatment)?
c.   Should immigrants who have entered the country illegally and worked here for years be granted citizenship?
d.   Should schools allow prayer or support events related to religious celebrations?
e.   Should the government pay college fees for all students who qualify?
f.   What is the best way to eliminate poverty in this nation?
3.   This is only the first step in the critical thinking process, followed by *assessing* the facts and *asserting* a concluding opinion.

D.   Instructions for Students
For the question being addressed, at your instructor's directions, respond to the following queries?

1.   How would you answer the question being addressed?
2.   What is your initial opinion regarding this issue?

---

[8] See CSWE (2008) *EPAS* EP 2.1.3. ("Apply critical thinking to inform and communicate professional judgments").
[9] See CSWE (2008) *EPAS* EP 2.1.2. ("Apply social work ethical principles to guide professional practice").
[10] See *EPAS* EP 2.1.2.
[11] See *EPAS* EP 2.1.2.

3. Upon what information do you base this opinion?

4. What are the potential positive and negative consequences if your opinion would be implemented?

5. Using critical thinking and the Triple A approach, what further questions might you ask to get accurate information about the issue?

6. What possible information would make you rethink your opinion? (The following are examples. If the answer was "yes" to question a, many people who have been put to death have later been found innocent. If "yes" to question b, consider the potential effects on people you know such as parents or grandparents. If "no" to question c, if parents of young children are sent back to their home country, should their children who were born here and are citizens remain behind?)

7. What professional social work values might apply concerning what the answer should be?

REFERENCES

Council on Social Work Education (CSWE). (2008). *Educational policy and accreditation standards (EPAS)*. Alexandria, VA: Author. (Available at www.cswe.org.)

Gitterman, A., & Germain, C. B. (2008). *The life model of social work practice* (3rd ed.). New York: Columbia.

Kirst-Ashman, K. K., & Hull, G. H., Jr. (2012). *Generalist practice with organizations and communities* (5th ed.). Belmont, CA: Brooks/Cole.

Payne, M. (2005). *Modern social work theory* (3rd ed.). Chicago: Lyceum.

Zastrow, C. H. & Kirst-Ashman, K. K. (2013). *Understanding human behavior and the social environment* (9th ed.). Belmont, CA: Brooks/Cole.

Chapter 1 Competencies/Practice Behaviors Exercises Assessment:

Name: _____ **Date:** _____
Supervisor's Name: _____

Focus Competencies/Practice Behaviors:
- EP 2.1.1b   Practice personal reflection and self-correction to assure continual professional development
- EP 2.1.2a   Recognize and manage personal values in a way that allows professional values to guide practice
- EP 2.1.3a   Distinguish, appraise, and integrate multiple sources of knowledge, including research-based knowledge and practice wisdom
- EP 2.1.4c   Recognize and communicate their understanding of the importance of difference in shaping life experiences
- EP 2.1.7a   Utilize conceptual frameworks to guide the processes of assessment, intervention, and evaluation
- EP 2.1.7b   Critique and apply knowledge to understand person and environment
- EP 2.1.8a   Analyze, formulate, and advocate for policies that advance social well-being
- EP 2.1.9a   Continuously discover, appraise, and attend to changing locales, populations, scientific and technological developments, and emerging societal trends to provide relevant services
- EP 2.1.10a   Substantively and affectively prepare for action with individuals, families, groups, organizations, and communities

Instructions:
A.   Evaluate your work or your partner's work in the Focus Competencies/Practice Behaviors by completing the Competencies/Practice Behaviors Assessment form below
B.   What other Competencies/Practice Behaviors did you use to complete these Exercises? Be sure to record them in your assessments

1.	I have attained this competency/practice behavior (in the range of 81 to 100%)
2.	I have largely attained this competency/practice behavior (in the range of 61 to 80%)
3.	I have partially attained this competency/practice behavior (in the range of 41 to 60%)
4.	I have made a little progress in attaining this competency/practice behavior (in the range of 21 to 40%)
5.	I have made almost no progress in attaining this competency/practice behavior (in the range of 0 to 20%)

EPAS 2008 Core Competencies & Core Practice Behaviors	Student Self Assessment						Evaluator Feedback
Student and Evaluator Assessment Scale and Comments	0	1	2	3	4	5	Agree/Disagree/ Comments
EP 2.1.1 Identify as a Professional Social Worker and Conduct Oneself Accordingly:							
a. Advocate for client access to the services of social work							
b. Practice personal reflection and self-correction to assure continual professional development							
c. Attend to professional roles and boundaries							
d. Demonstrate professional demeanor in behavior, appearance, and communication							
e. Engage in career-long learning							
f. Use supervision and consultation							
EP 2.1.2 Apply Social Work Ethical Principles to Guide Professional Practice:							
a. Recognize and manage personal values in a way that allows professional values to guide practice							
b. Make ethical decisions by applying NASW Code of Ethics and, as applicable, of the IFSW/IASSW Ethics in Social Work, Statement of Principles							
c. Tolerate ambiguity in resolving ethical conflicts							
d. Apply strategies of ethical reasoning to arrive at principled decisions							
EP 2.1.3 Apply Critical Thinking to Inform and Communicate Professional Judgments:							
a. Distinguish, appraise, and integrate multiple sources of knowledge, including research-based knowledge and practice wisdom							
b. Analyze models of assessment, prevention, intervention, and evaluation							
c. Demonstrate effective oral and written communication in working with individuals, families, groups, organizations, communities, and colleagues							
EP 2.1.4 Engage Diversity and Difference in Practice:							
a. Recognize the extent to which a culture's structures and values may oppress, marginalize, alienate, or create or enhance privilege and power							
b. Gain sufficient self-awareness to eliminate the influence of personal biases and values in working with diverse groups							
c. Recognize and communicate their understanding of the importance of difference in shaping life experiences							
d. View themselves as learners and engage those with whom they work as informants							
EP 2.1.5 Advance Human Rights and Social and Economic Justice:							
a. Understand forms and mechanisms of oppression and discrimination							
b. Advocate for human rights and social and economic justice							
c. Engage in practices that advance social and economic justice							

15

EP 2.1.6 Engage in Research-Informed Practice and Practice-Informed Research:							
a. Use practice experience to inform scientific inquiry							
b. Use research evidence to inform practice							
EP 2.1.7 Apply Knowledge of Human Behavior and the Social Environment:							
a. Utilize conceptual frameworks to guide the processes of assessment, intervention, and evaluation							
b. Critique and apply knowledge to understand person and environment							
EP 2.1.8 Engage in Policy Practice to Advance Social and Economic Well-Being and to Deliver Effective Social Work Services:							
a. Analyze, formulate, and advocate for policies that advance social well-being							
b. Collaborate with colleagues and clients for effective policy action							
EP 2.1.9 Respond to Contexts that Shape Practice:							
a. Continuously discover, appraise, and attend to changing locales, populations, scientific and technological developments, and emerging societal trends to provide relevant services							
b. Provide leadership in promoting sustainable changes in service delivery and practice to improve the quality of social services							
EP 2.1.10 Engage, Assess, Intervene, and Evaluate with Individuals, Families, Groups, Organizations and Communities:							
a. Substantively and affectively prepare for action with individuals, families, groups, organizations, and communities							
b. Use empathy and other interpersonal skills							
c. Develop a mutually agreed-on focus of work and desired outcomes							
d. Collect, organize, and interpret client data							
e. Assess client strengths and limitations							
f. Develop mutually agreed-on intervention goals and objectives							
g. Select appropriate intervention strategies							
h. Initiate actions to achieve organizational goals							
i. Implement prevention interventions that enhance client capacities							
j. Help clients resolve problems							
k. Negotiate, mediate, and advocate for clients							
l. Facilitate transitions and endings							
m. Critically analyze, monitor, and evaluate interventions							

Chapter 2
Values and Principles that Guide Generalist Practice in the Macro Social Environment

---

Competencies/Practice Behaviors Exercise 2.1
Personal Values

Focus Competencies or Practice Behaviors:

- EP 2.1.1b   Practice personal reflection and self-correction to assure continual professional development
- EP 2.1.2a   Recognize and manage personal values in a way that allows professional values to guide practice

A.   Brief Description

In a full-class discussion, you will explore the answers to questions about your own values and ethical standards. You will then compare these to professional values and standards.

B.   Objectives

You will:

1.   "Recognize" some "personal values."[1]
2.   Assess how personal values compare with professional values.

C.   Procedure

1.   Review the content on professional values and ethical standards.
2.   The instructor will pose the following questions to the class for a full-class discussion:

    a.   What values are most important to you? Caring for others? Self-preservation? Charity? Fairness? Equality? Material possessions? Financial stability? Honesty? Loyalty? Freedom of speech?

    b.   How do you make decisions about what is right and what is wrong? Do you have a personal code of ethics that guides your behavior? Do you consider yourself more of an independent thinker? Or do you tend to follow the majority and usually do what you're told?

    c.   To what extent do your personal values comply with professional values and ethical standards? Where do they agree and disagree?

---

[1] See Council on Social Work Education (CSWE) (2008) *Educational Policy and Accreditation Standards (EPAS)* Educational Policy (EP) 2.1.2 ("Apply ethical principles to guide professional practice").

Focus Competencies or Practice Behaviors:

- EP 2.1.2b   Make ethical decisions by applying standards of the National Association of Social Workers Code of Ethics and, as applicable, of the International Federation of Social Workers/International Association of Schools of Social Work Ethics in Social Work, Statement of Principles
- EP 2.1.2c   Tolerate ambiguity in resolving ethical conflicts
- EP 2.1.2d   Apply strategies of ethical reasoning to arrive at principled decisions
- EP 2.1.3a   Distinguish, appraise, and integrate multiple sources of knowledge, including research-based knowledge and practice wisdom

A.   **Brief Description**

Using a small group format, you are asked to assess and address each of two ethical dilemmas in the context of the macro environment.

B.   **Objectives**

You will:

1.   Begin to "engage in ethical decision-making" by evaluating ethical dilemmas.[2]

2.   Propose possible solutions to these dilemmas.

C.   **Procedure**

1.   Review the content on professional values, ethical standards, and ethical dilemmas.

2.   The class will be divided into small groups of four to six.

3.   The scenarios below will be presented to the class one at a time.

4.   The groups will answer and discuss the questions following each scenario. (You will also select a group representative who should be prepared to report to the entire class the small groups' findings.)

5.   After about 10 minutes for each scenario's small group discussion, the small groups will terminate their discussions and participate in a full-class discussion.

6.   A representative from each group will share her or his summary of the discussion. Comments from others in class will be encouraged. You will be asked about your reaction when pressed to address ethical dilemmas.

D.   **Instructions for Students**

Consider the following two examples occurring in the macro social environment and answer the subsequent questions. Your instructor will then lead a full-class discussion concerning your answers.

---

[2] See *EPAS* EP 2.1.2.

Scenario a: One practitioner, Bruce, reflects on his predicament: "I work in an agency that is not providing the services agreed to in exchange for grant money. Its brochures advertise the services as available and the agency documentation shows the services as provided, so the grantor believes the services are in place. The staff doesn't have the necessary resources, so those directly responsible for the care of the individuals who should be receiving the services are under a lot of stress. The consumers were promised something and are not getting it" (Kenyon, 1999, p. 213).

Answer the following questions:
- *What major issues are involved here?*
- *What alternatives are available to Bruce?*
- *What are the pros and cons of each alternative?*
- *What do you think is the "right thing" to do?*
- *What would you do if you were Bruce?*

Scenario b: "Adriana works in a community mental health clinic, and most of her time is devoted to dealing with immediate crises. The more she works with people in crisis, the more she is convinced that the focus of her work should be on preventive programs designed to educate the public. Adriana comes to believe strongly that there would be far fewer clients in distress if people were effectively contacted and motivated to participate in growth-oriented educational programs. She develops detailed, logical, and convincing proposals for programs she would like to implement in the community, but these proposals are consistently rejected by the director of her center. Because the clinic is partially funded by the government for the express purpose of crisis intervention, the director feels uneasy about approving any program that does not relate directly to this objective" (Corey, Corey, & Callanan, 2011, p. 533).

Answer the following questions:
- *What major issues are involved here?*
- *What alternatives are available to Adriana?*
- *What are the pros and cons of each alternative?*
- *What do you think is the "right thing" to do?*
- *What would you do if you were Adriana?*

Competencies/Practice Behaviors Exercise 2.3
Issues in Diversity

Focus Competencies or Practice Behaviors:
- EP 2.1.1b   Practice personal reflection and self-correction to assure continual professional development
- EP 2.1.2a   Recognize and manage personal values in a way that allows professional values to guide practice

- EP 2.1.4b   Gain sufficient self-awareness to eliminate the influence of personal biases and values in working with diverse groups
- EP 2.1.7b   Critique and apply knowledge to understand person and environment

A.   **Brief Description**

You will respond to questions about diversity, culture, and worldview in a full-class discussion.

B.   **Objectives**

You will:

1.   Begin to recognize and "understand how diversity characterizes and shapes the human experience."[3]

2.   "Critique and apply knowledge [about human diversity] to understand person and environment."[4]

3.   "Recognize … personal values" and perspectives concerning human diversity.[5]

4.   Evaluate the extent to which your personal values and perspectives comply with professional values.

C.   **Procedure**

1.   Review the content on human diversity, culture, cultural competence, and worldview.

2.   The following questions will be asked to the class.

a.   What are your thoughts about the value of human diversity? Is it some vague concept that is difficult to relate to? Do you think of specific groups of people?

b.   Are there any groups about whom you harbor some negative feelings? For example, people with physical or cognitive disabilities, older adults, people affiliated with certain religious organizations or sects, those with other racial backgrounds than your own, migrants or illegal immigrants, or people with a sexual orientation other than yours? If so, what are these negative perceptions? To what extent is it fair or reasonable to embrace these observations?

c.   How would you describe your own worldview? What are the major values and beliefs that support this worldview? To what extent does your worldview comply with professional social work values?

---

[3] See *EPAS* EP 2.1.4 ("Engage diversity and difference in practice").

[4] See *EPAS* EP 2.1.7 ("Apply knowledge of human behavior and the social environment").

[5] See *EPAS* EP 2.1.2

Competencies/Practice Behaviors Exercise 2.4
What are Your Strengths?

Focus Competencies or Practice Behaviors:
- EP 2.1.1b   Practice personal reflection and self-correction to assure continual professional development
- EP 2.1.10d   Collect, organize, and interpret client data
- EP 2.1.10e   Assess client strengths and limitations

A.   Brief Description

You will be given a questionnaire and asked to identify your strengths ranging from personal strong points to relationships and support in the macro social environment.

B.   Objectives

You will:

1.   Identify a range of personal strengths at the micro, mezzo, and macro levels.

2.   Relate your own range of strengths to those of your clients in order to prepare you to "assess client strengths and limitations" in practice.[6]

C.   Procedure

1.   Handouts of the questionnaire posed below will be distributed to the class.

2.   You will have about 10 minutes to fill it out. Ask questions if you don't understand what the questions mean.

3.   After you have completed the questionnaire, the instructor will initiate a classroom discussion regarding what you reported for each level of strengths.

4.   Discuss how the identification of your own strengths might give you insight into identifying and using your clients' strengths at micro, mezzo, and macro levels.

D.   Instructions for Students

Answer the following questions regarding your strengths at the micro, mezzo, and macro levels. (Feel free to ask your instructor if you don't understand exactly what the question means.) Your instructor will then lead a full-class discussion concerning your answers.

Individual Strengths:
-   *What do you see as your most significant personal strengths?*
-   *What challenges have you overcome about which you're especially proud?*

---

[6] See *EPAS* EP 2.1.10d ("collect, organize, and interpret client data") and 2.1.10e ("assess client strengths and limitations").

Family Strengths:
- *What strengths do you see in your own family?*
- *In what ways does your family put these strengths to use?*
- *In times of trouble, how does your family contribute to your own personal sense of strength?*

Group Strengths:
- *To what social, work, and other types of groups do you belong?*
- *Do you have special people upon whom you can rely? If so, who are they and in what ways do they support you?*
- *What are the strengths inherent in these groups?*
- *How do these group strengths contribute to your own personal sense of strength?*

Organizational Strengths:
- *To what organizations do you belong (for example, clubs, work settings, churches, recreational groups, sports groups, volunteer groups)?*
- *What are the strengths of these organizations?*
- *How do these organizational strengths and your organizational membership contribute to your own personal sense of strength?*

Community Strengths:
- *What are the strengths in the community where you live?*
- *How do these strengths contribute to your own quality of life?*

Competencies/Practice Behaviors Exercise 2.5
Role Play—Global Oppression and Human Rights

Focus Competencies or Practice Behaviors:
- EP 2.1.1b Practice personal reflection and self-correction to assure continual professional development
- EP 2.1.2a Recognize and manage personal values in a way that allows professional values to guide practice
- EP 2.1.3a Distinguish, appraise, and integrate multiple sources of knowledge, including research-based knowledge and practice wisdom
- EP 2.1.4a Recognize the extent to which a culture's structures and values may oppress, marginalize, alienate, or create or enhance privilege and power
- EP 2.1.4b Gain sufficient self-awareness to eliminate the influence of personal biases and values in working with diverse groups
- EP 2.1.5a Understand forms and mechanisms of oppression and discrimination
- EP 2.1.5b Advocate for human rights and social and economic justice
- EP 2.1.5c Engage in practices that advance social and economic justice

A. **Brief Description**

In a full-class discussion, you will explore the answers to questions about your own values and ethical standards. You will then compare these to professional values and standards.

B. **Objectives**

You will:

1. "Recognize" some "personal values"[7] about "oppression, poverty, marginalization, and alienation as well as privilege, power, and acclaim."[8]
2. Assess how personal values compare with professional values.

C. **Procedure**

1. Review the content on advocacy for human rights, and social and economic justice including the concepts of oppression, power, privilege, acclaim, marginalization, alienation, poverty, populations-at-risk, stereotypes, and discrimination.
2. The following questions will be posed to the class for a full-class discussion:

    a. Do you have thoughts about the status of human rights in the world today?

    b. Globally, do oppressed populations exist? If so, who are they?

    c. What do you think are the causes of oppression? How do you think the concepts we discussed are involved in oppression? Should oppression be stopped? Can it be? If so, how should it be stopped? Who should stop it?

---

[7] See *EPAS* EP 2.1.2.
[8] See *EPAS* EP 2.1.4.

REFERENCES

Corey, G., Corey, M. S., & Callanan, P. (2011). *Issues and ethics in the helping professions* (8th ed.). Belmont, CA: Brooks/Cole.

Council on Social Work Education (CSWE). (2008). *Educational policy and accreditation standards (EPAS)*. Alexandria, VA: Author. (Available at www.cswe.org.)

Kenyon, P. (1999). What would you do? *An ethical case workbook for human service professionals*. Belmont, CA: Brooks/Cole.

Chapter 2 Competencies/Practice Behaviors Exercises Assessment:

Name: _____ **Date:** _____

Supervisor's Name: _____

Focus Competencies/Practice Behaviors:

- EP 2.1.1b   Practice personal reflection and self-correction to assure continual professional development
- EP 2.1.2a   Recognize and manage personal values in a way that allows professional values to guide practice
- EP 2.1.2b   Make ethical decisions by applying standards of the National Association of Social Workers Code of Ethics and, as applicable, of the International Federation of Social Workers/International Association of Schools of Social Work Ethics in Social Work, Statement of Principles
- EP 2.1.2c   Tolerate ambiguity in resolving ethical conflicts
- EP 2.1.2d   Apply strategies of ethical reasoning to arrive at principled decisions
- EP 2.1.3a   Distinguish, appraise, and integrate multiple sources of knowledge, including research-based knowledge and practice wisdom
- EP 2.1.4a   Recognize the extent to which a culture's structures and values may oppress, marginalize, alienate, or create or enhance privilege and power
- EP 2.1.4b   Gain sufficient self-awareness to eliminate the influence of personal biases and values in working with diverse groups
- EP 2.1.5a   Understand forms and mechanisms of oppression and discrimination
- EP 2.1.5b   Advocate for human rights and social and economic justice
- EP 2.1.5c   Engage in practices that advance social and economic justice
- EP 2.1.7b   Critique and apply knowledge to understand person and environment
- EP 2.1.10d   Collect, organize, and interpret client data
- EP 2.1.10e   Assess client strengths and limitations

Instructions:

A.   Evaluate your work or your partner's work in the Focus Competencies/Practice Behaviors by completing the Competencies/Practice Behaviors Assessment form below

B.   What other Competencies/Practice Behaviors did you use to complete these Exercises? Be sure to record them in your assessments

1.	I have attained this competency/practice behavior (in the range of 81 to 100%)
2.	I have largely attained this competency/practice behavior (in the range of 61 to 80%)
3.	I have partially attained this competency/practice behavior (in the range of 41 to 60%)
4.	I have made a little progress in attaining this competency/practice behavior (in the range of 21 to 40%)
5.	I have made almost no progress in attaining this competency/practice behavior (in the range of 0 to 20%)

EPAS 2008 Core Competencies & Core Practice Behaviors	Student Self Assessment						Evaluator Feedback
Student and Evaluator Assessment Scale and Comments	0	1	2	3	4	5	Agree/Disagree/Comments
EP 2.1.1 Identify as a Professional Social Worker and Conduct Oneself Accordingly:							
a. Advocate for client access to the services of social work							
b. Practice personal reflection and self-correction to assure continual professional development							
c. Attend to professional roles and boundaries							
d. Demonstrate professional demeanor in behavior, appearance, and communication							
e. Engage in career-long learning							
f. Use supervision and consultation							
EP 2.1.2 Apply Social Work Ethical Principles to Guide Professional Practice:							
a. Recognize and manage personal values in a way that allows professional values to guide practice							
b. Make ethical decisions by applying NASW Code of Ethics and, as applicable, of the IFSW/IASSW Ethics in Social Work, Statement of Principles							
c. Tolerate ambiguity in resolving ethical conflicts							
d. Apply strategies of ethical reasoning to arrive at principled decisions							
EP 2.1.3 Apply Critical Thinking to Inform and Communicate Professional Judgments:							
a. Distinguish, appraise, and integrate multiple sources of knowledge, including research-based knowledge and practice wisdom							
b. Analyze models of assessment, prevention, intervention, and evaluation							
c. Demonstrate effective oral and written communication in working with individuals, families, groups, organizations, communities, and colleagues							
EP 2.1.4 Engage Diversity and Difference in Practice:							
a. Recognize the extent to which a culture's structures and values may oppress, marginalize, alienate, or create or enhance privilege and power							
b. Gain sufficient self-awareness to eliminate the influence of personal biases and values in working with diverse groups							
c. Recognize and communicate their understanding of the importance of difference in shaping life experiences							
d. View themselves as learners and engage those with whom they work as informants							
EP 2.1.5 Advance Human Rights and Social and Economic Justice:							
a. Understand forms and mechanisms of oppression and discrimination							

b. Advocate for human rights and social and economic justice							
c. Engage in practices that advance social and economic justice							
EP 2.1.6 Engage in Research-Informed Practice and Practice-Informed Research:							
a. Use practice experience to inform scientific inquiry							
b. Use research evidence to inform practice							
EP 2.1.7 Apply Knowledge of Human Behavior and the Social Environment:							
a. Utilize conceptual frameworks to guide the processes of assessment, intervention, and evaluation							
b. Critique and apply knowledge to understand person and environment							
EP 2.1.8 Engage in Policy Practice to Advance Social and Economic Well-Being and to Deliver Effective Social Work Services:							
a. Analyze, formulate, and advocate for policies that advance social well-being							
b. Collaborate with colleagues and clients for effective policy action							
EP 2.1.9 Respond to Contexts that Shape Practice:							
a. Continuously discover, appraise, and attend to changing locales, populations, scientific and technological developments, and emerging societal trends to provide relevant services							
b. Provide leadership in promoting sustainable changes in service delivery and practice to improve the quality of social services							
EP 2.1.10 Engage, Assess, Intervene, and Evaluate with Individuals, Families, Groups, Organizations and Communities:							
a. Substantively and affectively prepare for action with individuals, families, groups, organizations, and communities							
b. Use empathy and other interpersonal skills							
c. Develop a mutually agreed-on focus of work and desired outcomes							
d. Collect, organize, and interpret client data							
e. Assess client strengths and limitations							
f. Develop mutually agreed-on intervention goals and objectives							
g. Select appropriate intervention strategies							
h. Initiate actions to achieve organizational goals							
i. Implement prevention interventions that enhance client capacities							
j. Help clients resolve problems							
k. Negotiate, mediate, and advocate for clients							
l. Facilitate transitions and endings							
m. Critically analyze, monitor, and evaluate interventions							

Competencies/Practice Behaviors Exercise 3.1
Theoretical Debate

Focus Competencies or Practice Behaviors:

- EP 2.1.1   Identify as a professional social worker and conduct oneself accordingly
- EP 2.1.3a   Distinguish, appraise, and integrate multiple sources of knowledge, including research-based knowledge and practice wisdom
- EP 2.1.7a   Utilize conceptual frameworks to guide the processes of assessment, intervention, and evaluation
- EP 2.1.7b   Critique and apply knowledge to understand person and environment

A.   **Brief Description**

In small groups you will be asked to discuss seven theories or conceptual frameworks on groups. Then you will be asked to summarize major concepts and evaluate the strengths and weaknesses of each perspective in the context of social work practice.

B.   **Objectives**

You will:

1.   Identify major concepts inherent in the seven identified "conceptual frameworks" concerning small groups as "social systems in which people live."[1]

2.   "Critique and apply knowledge [about groups] to understand person and environment."[2]

3.   Evaluate the appropriateness and relevance of each framework as a guide to "the processes of assessment, intervention, and evaluation" in social work practice.[3]

C.   **Procedure**

1.   Review the five conceptual frameworks on groups *(field, social exchange, learning, psychoanalytic, systems, empowerment,* and *feminist theories)* before beginning the activity.

2.   In small groups you will be asked to summarize the major concepts inherent in each of the perspectives and then will be given several questions to address concerning the theories. At least one group member should take notes regarding major discussion points. At the end of about

---

[1] See Council on Social Work Education (CSWE) *Educational Policy and Accreditation Standards (EPAS)* Educational Policy (EP) 2.1.7, ("Apply knowledge of human behavior and the social environment").

[2] See *EPAS* EP 2.1.7.

[3] See *EPAS* EP 2.1.7.

20 minutes you will return to a full-class discussion where note-takers and other group participants will be asked to report your findings.

D.   Instructions for Students
Within your small groups:
1.   Summarize the major concepts involved in each of the five theoretical perspectives. It's helpful to have a visual aid such as PowerPoint or a handout.
2.   Subsequently, discuss the following questions with respect to each theoretical perspective:
   a.   How does this theoretical perspective apply well to treatment and task groups in social work practice? What specific concepts inherent in the theory fit well?
   b.   In what ways is it difficult to apply this theoretical perspective to treatment and task groups in social work practice? What specific concepts inherent in the theory fit poorly?
   c.   What theory or theories do you think make the most sense and why?

Competencies/Practice Behaviors Exercise 3.2
Are You A Feminist?

Focus Competencies or Practice Behaviors:
- EP 2.1.1b   Practice personal reflection and self-correction to assure continual professional development
- EP 2.1.2a   Recognize and manage personal values in a way that allows professional values to guide practice
- EP 2.1.4a   Recognize the extent to which a culture's structures and values may oppress, marginalize, alienate, or create or enhance privilege and power
- EP 2.1.4b   Gain sufficient self-awareness to eliminate the influence of personal biases and values in working with diverse groups
- EP 2.1.4c   Recognize and communicate their understanding of the importance of difference in shaping life experiences
- EP 2.1.4d   View themselves as learners and engage those with whom they work as informants
- EP 2.1.5a   Understand forms and mechanisms of oppression and discrimination
- EP 2.1.7a   Utilize conceptual frameworks to guide the processes of assessment, intervention, and evaluation
- EP 2.1.7b   Critique and apply knowledge to understand person and environment

A.	**Brief Description**
You will answer a questionnaire regarding feminism and discuss your values concerning the issue.

B.	**Objectives**
You will:
1.	"Critique and apply knowledge [about gender and feminism] to understand person and environment."[4]
2.	Explore "how diversity [in terms of gender] characterizes and shapes the human experience and is critical to the formation of identity."[5]
3.	Assess the concepts inherent in feminist theories.
4.	Begin to "recognize ... personal values in a way that allows professional values to guide practice" concerning gender issues.[6]
5.	"View themselves as learners" concerning issues related to gender.[7]

C.	**Procedure**
1.	Review the content on feminist theories including the following concepts:
	a.	Using a gender filter.
	b.	Assuming a pro-woman perspective.
	c.	Empowerment.
	d.	Consciousness raising.
	e.	The "personal is political" (Bricker-Jenkins & Netting, 2009, p. 279).
	f.	The importance of process.
	g.	Unity in diversity; "diversity is strength" (Gutierrez & Lewis, 1999, p. 105).
	h.	Validation.
2.	The questionnaire depicted below will be distributed and you will be asked to fill it out.
3.	After you've completed the questionnaire, a discussion will be initiated that reviews your answers question by question. You will be encouraged to share the reasons for your answers.
4.	Subsequently, a discussion will be led with the entire class that addresses the following questions and issues:
	a.	Are you or are you not a feminist? Explain why or why not.
	b.	How would you define feminism using your own words?
	c.	What negative images does feminism conjure up for many people?
	d.	To what extent do feminist principles contradict or coincide with professional social work values?
	e.	What insights, if any, have you gained from this discussion? Do you view yourself as a future learner of new ideas concerning these issues?

---

[4] See *EPAS* EP 2.1.7.
[5] See *EPAS* EP 2.1.4 ("Engage diversity and difference in practice").
[6] See *EPAS* EP 2.1.2 ("Apply social work ethical principles to guide professional practice").
[7] See *EPAS* EP 2.1.4.

f. Have your views about these issues changed over time?
g. Do you foresee how your views might change in the future as you gain more information, knowledge, and experience?

D.   Instructions for Students

1. Complete the following questionnaire after which your instructor will lead a discussion concerning your answers.

Questionnaire:
Are You a Feminist?

a. Do you believe that women should have the same rights as men?
☐ Yes   ☐ No

b. Do you believe that women should have the same access to jobs and social status as men?
☐ Yes   ☐ No

c. Do you believe that women should *not* be discriminated against or *denied* opportunities and choices on the basis of their gender?
☐ Yes   ☐ No

d. Do you believe that, ideally, people's attitudes and behavior should reflect the equal treatment of women?
☐ Yes   ☐ No

e. Do you think that many people need to become more educated about women's issues?
☐ Yes   ☐ No

f. Would you be willing to advocate on behalf of women (for instance, for poor women or women who have been raped)?
☐ Yes   ☐ No

g. Do you believe that both men and women have the right to their own individual differences (that is, of course, differences which don't harm other people)?
☐ Yes   ☐ No

h. Do you think that our society is generally structured legally, socially, and economically by and for men instead of women?
☐ Yes   ☐ No

---

2. Count the number of times you answered "yes" to the eight questions.
3. Your instructor will lead a discussion with the entire class that reviews your answers to each of the questionnaire's questions and subsequently addresses additional questions and issues.

Competencies/Practice Behaviors Exercise 3.3
Power Sources

Focus Competencies or Practice Behaviors:
- EP 2.1.4a   Recognize the extent to which a culture's structures and values may oppress, marginalize, alienate, or create or enhance privilege and power
- EP 2.1.7b   Critique and apply knowledge to understand person and environment

A.   **Brief Description**
You will be presented with six scenarios and asked to determine what types of power sources apply.

B.   **Objectives**
You will:
1.   Identify the five types of power sources.
2.   "Critique and apply knowledge [about power] to understand person and environment" by appraising what power sources are evident in a range of scenarios.[8]

C.   **Procedure**
1.   Review the content on sources of power in groups (legitimate, reward, coercive, referent, and expert).
2.   Discuss the six scenarios posed below regarding what power sources apply to each and why.

D.   **Instructions for Students**
1.   Discuss what types of power *(legitimate, reward, coercive, referent,* and *expert)* are reflected in the following situations and why:
     a.   Forrest Gump, an army private serving in the 1960s Vietnam war, saves his wounded colleagues by carrying them from the battleground under attack to safety.
     b.   An ophthalmologist who specializes in retinal transplants determines whether a patient would benefit from surgery or not.
     c.   One of your instructors informs the class that no students will probably be capable of getting an "A" in the class. You are not impressed, nor do you have much respect for this instructor's capabilities.
     d.   You have been invited to attend a Governor's dinner party as a student representative of your social work program. The Governor is not of the political party you support.

---

[8] See *EPAS* EP 2.1.4.

e.   Your boss, the assistant manager at Petey's Pizza Palace, gives you a hefty raise for performance in your part-time job. You respect her and feel she has good communication skills.

f.   A famous poet signs copies of his most recently published book at one of his presentations that you attend. You really don't care for his poetry very much and are not at all interested in getting his autograph.

Competencies/Practice Behaviors Exercise 3.4
You and Your Leadership Potential

Focus Competencies or Practice Behaviors:

- EP 2.1.1b   Practice personal reflection and self-correction to assure continual professional development
- EP 2.1.9b   Provide leadership in promoting sustainable changes in service delivery and practice to improve the quality of social services

A.   Brief Description

You will answer a questionnaire regarding your own leadership ability and subsequently identify means of developing and improving leadership skills.

B.   Objectives

You will:

1. Explore your own strengths and weaknesses related to leadership ability.
2. Identify how you might improve your leadership skills.

C.   Procedure

1. Review the content on leadership in task groups.
2. Fill it out the following questionnaire.
3. Discuss your perceptions of your own strengths and weaknesses related to leadership ability. Address the following questions:
   a.   What do you see as your strengths and weaknesses concerning leadership ability?
   b.   What do you feel are the most important qualities inherent in an effective leader?
   c.   What leaders can you think of that have demonstrated effective leadership ability? In what ways have they done so? What qualities do they exhibit?
   d.   How might an individual develop and improve leadership skills? Through activities? Interactions? Experiences?

D.   Instructions for Students

1. Complete the following questionnaire after which your instructor will initiate a class discussion.

LEADERSHIP QUESTIONNAIRE

How would you rate yourself on the following dimensions (1 being very poor and 10 being exceptional)?

a.   **Self-confidence**

1-----2----3----4----5----6----7----8----9----10
Very poor   Average   Exceptional

b.   **Self-concept**

1-----2----3----4----5----6----7----8----9----10
Very poor   Average   Exceptional

c.   **Humility**

1-----2----3----4----5----6----7----8----9----10
Very poor   Average   Exceptional

d.   **Intelligence**

1-----2----3----4----5----6----7----8----9----10
Very poor   Average   Exceptional

e.   **Determination**

1-----2----3----4----5----6----7----8----9----10
Very poor   Average   Exceptional

f.   **Trustworthiness**

1-----2----3----4----5----6----7----8----9----10
Very poor   Average   Exceptional

g.   **Integrity**

1-----2----3----4----5----6----7----8----9----10
Very poor   Average   Exceptional

h.   **Sociability**

1-----2----3----4----5----6----7----8----9----10
Very poor   Average   Exceptional

i.   **Emotional intelligence**

1-----2----3----4----5----6----7----8----9----10
Very poor   Average   Exceptional

j.   **Self-awareness**

1-----2----3----4----5----6----7----8----9----10
Very poor   Average   Exceptional

k.   **Self-management**

1-----2----3----4----5----6----7----8----9----10
Very poor   Average   Exceptional

l.   **Social awareness**

1-----2----3----4----5----6----7----8----9----10
Very poor   Average   Exceptional

m.   **Relationship management**

1-----2----3----4----5----6----7----8----9----10
Very poor   Average   Exceptional

n.   **Flexibility**

1-----2----3----4----5----6----7----8----9----10
Very poor   Average   Exceptional

2.   Add up your total score and divide by 14. This may provide some insight into how you view your own leadership potential. A lower score would indicate having limitations and a higher score would reveal strengths. Reviewing the score of each dimension could help indicate what areas you might work on to improve your leadership ability.

REFERENCES

Bricker-Jenkins, M., & Netting, F. E. (2009). Feminist issues and practices in social work. In A. R. Roberts (Editor-in-Chief), *Social workers' desk reference* (2nd ed., pp. 277-283). New York: Oxford.

Council on Social Work Education (CSWE). (2008). *Educational policy and accreditation standards (EPAS)*. Alexandria, VA: Author. (Available at www.cswe.org.)

Gutierrez, L. M., & Lewis, E. A. (1999). *Empowering women of color*. New York: Columbia.

Chapter 3 Competencies/Practice Behaviors Exercises Assessment:

Name: _____ **Date:** _____
Supervisor's Name: _____

Focus Competencies/Practice Behaviors:

- EP 2.1.1   Identify as a professional social worker and conduct oneself accordingly
- EP 2.1.1b   Practice personal reflection and self-correction to assure continual professional development
- EP 2.1.2a   Recognize and manage personal values in a way that allows professional values to guide practice
- EP 2.1.3a   Distinguish, appraise, and integrate multiple sources of knowledge, including research-based knowledge and practice wisdom
- EP 2.1.4a   Recognize the extent to which a culture's structures and values may oppress, marginalize, alienate, or create or enhance privilege and power
- EP 2.1.4b   Gain sufficient self-awareness to eliminate the influence of personal biases and values in working with diverse groups
- EP 2.1.4c   Recognize and communicate their understanding of the importance of difference in shaping life experiences
- EP 2.1.4d   View themselves as learners and engage those with whom they work as informants
- EP 2.1.5a   Understand forms and mechanisms of oppression and discrimination
- EP 2.1.7a   Utilize conceptual frameworks to guide the processes of assessment, intervention, and evaluation
- EP 2.1.7b   Critique and apply knowledge to understand person and environment
- EP 2.1.9b   Provide leadership in promoting sustainable changes in service delivery and practice to improve the quality of social services

Instructions:

A.   Evaluate your work or your partner's work in the Focus Competencies/Practice Behaviors by completing the Competencies/Practice Behaviors Assessment form below

B.   What other Competencies/Practice Behaviors did you use to complete these Exercises? Be sure to record them in your assessments

1.	I have attained this competency/practice behavior (in the range of 81 to 100%)
2.	I have largely attained this competency/practice behavior (in the range of 61 to 80%)
3.	I have partially attained this competency/practice behavior (in the range of 41 to 60%)
4.	I have made a little progress in attaining this competency/practice behavior (in the range of 21 to 40%)
5.	I have made almost no progress in attaining this competency/practice behavior (in the range of 0 to 20%)

EPAS 2008 Core Competencies & Core Practice Behaviors	Student Self Assessment						Evaluator Feedback
Student and Evaluator Assessment Scale and Comments	0	1	2	3	4	5	Agree/Disagree/ Comments
EP 2.1.1 Identify as a Professional Social Worker and Conduct Oneself Accordingly:							
a. Advocate for client access to the services of social work							
b. Practice personal reflection and self-correction to assure continual professional development							
c. Attend to professional roles and boundaries							
d. Demonstrate professional demeanor in behavior, appearance, and communication							
e. Engage in career-long learning							
f. Use supervision and consultation							
EP 2.1.2 Apply Social Work Ethical Principles to Guide Professional Practice:							
a. Recognize and manage personal values in a way that allows professional values to guide practice							
b. Make ethical decisions by applying NASW Code of Ethics and, as applicable, of the IFSW/IASSW Ethics in Social Work, Statement of Principles							
c. Tolerate ambiguity in resolving ethical conflicts							
d. Apply strategies of ethical reasoning to arrive at principled decisions							
EP 2.1.3 Apply Critical Thinking to Inform and Communicate Professional Judgments:							
a. Distinguish, appraise, and integrate multiple sources of knowledge, including research-based knowledge and practice wisdom							
b. Analyze models of assessment, prevention, intervention, and evaluation							
c. Demonstrate effective oral and written communication in working with individuals, families, groups, organizations, communities, and colleagues							
EP 2.1.4 Engage Diversity and Difference in Practice:							
a. Recognize the extent to which a culture's structures and values may oppress, marginalize, alienate, or create or enhance privilege and power							
b. Gain sufficient self-awareness to eliminate the influence of personal biases and values in working with diverse groups							
c. Recognize and communicate their understanding of the importance of difference in shaping life experiences							
d. View themselves as learners and engage those with whom they work as informants							
EP 2.1.5 Advance Human Rights and Social and Economic Justice:							
a. Understand forms and mechanisms of oppression and discrimination							
b. Advocate for human rights and social and economic justice							
c. Engage in practices that advance social and economic justice							

EP 2.1.6 Engage in Research-Informed Practice and Practice-Informed Research:								
a.	Use practice experience to inform scientific inquiry							
b.	Use research evidence to inform practice							
EP 2.1.7 Apply Knowledge of Human Behavior and the Social Environment:								
a.	Utilize conceptual frameworks to guide the processes of assessment, intervention, and evaluation							
b.	Critique and apply knowledge to understand person and environment							
EP 2.1.8 Engage in Policy Practice to Advance Social and Economic Well-Being and to Deliver Effective Social Work Services:								
a.	Analyze, formulate, and advocate for policies that advance social well-being							
b.	Collaborate with colleagues and clients for effective policy action							
EP 2.1.9 Respond to Contexts that Shape Practice:								
a.	Continuously discover, appraise, and attend to changing locales, populations, scientific and technological developments, and emerging societal trends to provide relevant services							
b.	Provide leadership in promoting sustainable changes in service delivery and practice to improve the quality of social services							
EP 2.1.10 Engage, Assess, Intervene, and Evaluate with Individuals, Families, Groups, Organizations and Communities:								
a.	Substantively and affectively prepare for action with individuals, families, groups, organizations, and communities							
b.	Use empathy and other interpersonal skills							
c.	Develop a mutually agreed-on focus of work and desired outcomes							
d.	Collect, organize, and interpret client data							
e.	Assess client strengths and limitations							
f.	Develop mutually agreed-on intervention goals and objectives							
g.	Select appropriate intervention strategies							
h.	Initiate actions to achieve organizational goals							
i.	Implement prevention interventions that enhance client capacities							
j.	Help clients resolve problems							
k.	Negotiate, mediate, and advocate for clients							
l.	Facilitate transitions and endings							
m.	Critically analyze, monitor, and evaluate interventions							

Chapter 4
Types of Groups in the Macro Social Environment

Competencies/Practice Behaviors Exercise 4.1
Identifying Types of Groups

Focus Competencies or Practice Behaviors:
- EP 2.1.5c   Engage in practices that advance social and economic justice
- EP 2.1.7   Apply knowledge of human behavior and the social environment
- EP 2.1.8a   Analyze, formulate, and advocate for policies that advance social well-being
- EP 2.1.8b   Collaborate with colleagues and clients for effective policy action
- EP 2.1.9b   Provide leadership in promoting sustainable changes in service delivery and practice to improve the quality of social services
- EP 2.1.10a   Substantively and affectively prepare for action with individuals, families, groups, organizations, and communities
- EP 2.1.10h   Initiate actions to achieve organizational goals

A.   **Brief Description**
      You are asked to match types of treatment groups with their respective definitions, examine similarities and difficulties, and propose appropriate agency settings and client populations.

B.   **Objectives**
      You will:
      1.   Recognize types of task and treatment groups as part of "the range of social systems in which people live," identify the primary concepts characterizing each group, and examine the various groups' similarities and differences.[1]
      2.   Propose appropriate agency settings and client populations for each.
      3.   "Critique and apply knowledge [about various types of groups] to understand person and environment."[2]

C.   **Procedure**
      1.   You will be given a handout with the information below under "D. Instructions for Students."

---

[1] See Council on Social Work Education (CSWE) *Educational Policy and Accreditation Standards (EPAS)* Educational Policy (EP) 2.1.7, ("Apply knowledge of human behavior and the social environment").
[2] See *EPAS* EP 2.1.7.

2. The instructor will either have you form small groups for discussion or will ask you individually to match the type of treatment group with the appropriate description.

3. The subsequent questions will be posed as a basis for a full-class discussion.

D. Instructions for Students

1. Match the following types of groups with the respective descriptions:

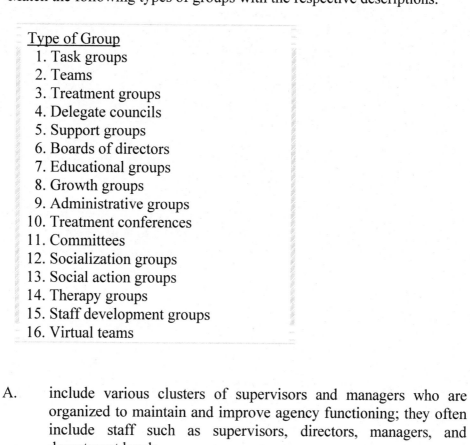

Type of Group
1. Task groups
2. Teams
3. Treatment groups
4. Delegate councils
5. Support groups
6. Boards of directors
7. Educational groups
8. Growth groups
9. Administrative groups
10. Treatment conferences
11. Committees
12. Socialization groups
13. Social action groups
14. Therapy groups
15. Staff development groups
16. Virtual teams

_____ A. include various clusters of supervisors and managers who are organized to maintain and improve agency functioning; they often include staff such as supervisors, directors, managers, and department heads.

_____ B. are groups of elected or appointed representatives from a series of agencies or units within a single agency who serve to achieve such goals as enhancing cooperation among professionals in different units or agencies, reviewing issues relevant to service provision, or pursuing social action goals (Toseland & Rivas, 2012).

_____ C. are those aimed at expanding self-awareness, increasing self potential, and maximizing optimal health and well-being.

_____ D. help individuals solve personal problems, change unwanted behaviors, cope with stress, and improve group members' quality of life.

_____ E.   provide information to participants.

_____ F.   are groups of people authorized to formulate the organization's mission, objectives, and policies in addition to overseeing the organization's ongoing activities.

_____ G.   is a collection of people that applies the principles of group dynamics to solve problems, develop innovative ideas, formulate plans, and achieve goals.

_____ H.   are groups of people "delegated to consider, investigate, take action on, or report on some matter" (Mish, 2008, p. 250).

_____ I.   help participants improve interpersonal behavior, communication, and social skills so that they might better fit into their social environment.

_____ J.   are groups that meet to establish, monitor, and coordinate service plans on the behalf of a client system.

_____ K.   consist of participants who share common issues or problems and meet on an ongoing basis to cope with stress, give each other suggestions, provide encouragement, convey information, and furnish emotional support (Barker, 2003).

_____ L.   are groups of two or more people gathered together to work collaboratively and interdependently with each other to pursue a designated purpose.

_____ M.   are formed to engage in some planned change effort to shift power and resources in order to modify or improve aspects of their macro social or physical environment.

_____ N.   establish goals to improve, update, and refine workers' skills, the ultimate goal being to improve service to clients (Toseland & Rivas, 2012).

_____ O.   help members with serious psychological and emotional problems change their behavior; they are led by an expert whose emphasis is placed on "remediation and rehabilitation" (Toseland & Rivas, 2012, p. 25).

_____ P.   is "a small group of people who conduct almost all of their collaborative work by electronic communication rather than in face-to-face meetings" (Dubrin, 2012, p. 477).

2.	After matching, answer and respond to the following:
  a.	What concepts in the definitions characterize each group and make that group unique?
  b.	What are the similarities and differences among the groups?
  c.	Describe an agency setting where each group might be appropriate. Give specific examples of the type of problems and clientele each group might include. (For example, a committee might be formed in a county social services agency to address how offices are spaced and allocated within the agency, or a therapy group for bulimics might be held at a community counseling center.)

Competencies/Practice Behaviors Exercise 4.2
Critical Thinking about Parent Involvement in Treatment Conferences

---

Focus Competencies or Practice Behaviors:
- EP 2.1.1a	Advocate for client access to the services of social work
- EP 2.1.2	Apply social work ethical principles to guide professional practice
- EP 2.1.2b	Make ethical decisions by applying standards of the National Association of Social Workers Code of Ethics and, as applicable, of the International Federation of Social Workers/International Association of Schools of Social Work Ethics in Social Work, Statement of Principles
- EP 2.1.3	Apply critical thinking to inform and communicate professional judgments
- EP 2.1.3a	Distinguish, appraise, and integrate multiple sources of knowledge, including research-based knowledge and practice wisdom
- EP 2.1.5c	Engage in practices that advance social and economic justice
- EP 2.1.8a	Analyze, formulate, and advocate for policies that advance social well-being
- EP 2.1.8b	Collaborate with colleagues and clients for effective policy action
- EP 2.1.9b	Provide leadership in promoting sustainable changes in service delivery and practice to improve the quality of social services
- EP 2.1.10c	Develop a mutually agreed-on focus of work and desired outcomes
- EP 2.1.10f	Develop mutually agreed-on intervention goals and objectives

A.	**Brief Description**
  In small groups you are asked to discuss a case example involving an agency whose policy is to exclude clients' and their families' attendance at treatment conferences. Discussion focuses on the pros and cons of inclusion and exclusion, and the ethical implications for each kind of policy.

B. Objectives

You will:

1. Apply critical thinking skills to evaluate the importance of client involvement in agency practices such as treatment conferences.[3]
2. "Apply strategies of ethical reasoning to arrive at principled decisions" by proposing recommendations for ethical behavior on the part of the targeted agency.[4]

C. Procedure

1. Review the material on treatment conferences.
2. The class will be divided into small groups of four to six.
3. The scenario presented below will be read to the class.
4. The groups will be asked to discuss the subsequent questions, select a group representative, and be prepared to report to the entire class the small group's findings.
5. The small groups will be asked to terminate their discussions and participate in a large class discussion.
6. A representative from each group will be asked to share her or his summary of the discussion and comments from others will be encouraged.

D. Instructions for Students

1. Read the following scenario and respond to the ensuing questions.

SCENARIO: Proposed here is an example of a treatment conference in a diagnostic and treatment center for children with multiple physical and psychological disabilities. The client Timmy, 3, has severe cerebral palsy, a disability resulting from damage to the brain before, during, or shortly after birth that results in problems with muscular coordination and speech (Mish, 2008). Timmy has very little control of his extremities, torso, face, and mouth. He has some limited control of his eyes.

After Timmy is referred for assessment, extensive testing is performed by speech, occupational, and physical therapists. A physician conducts a thorough physical examination and orders relevant tests. Sometimes, a geneticist is involved to establish the etiology of the disorder. However, Timmy experienced oxygen deprivation at birth due to the umbilical cord being wrapped around his neck. Since the etiology of the disability has been established, the program director, a physician, determines that a genetic assessment is unnecessary. A psychologist conducts perceptual and ability testing. Finally, a social worker carries out a family assessment.

All evaluators subsequently attend the treatment conference. This particular group cannot be considered a team because it does not work together on a regular basis. For example, there are five occupational therapists and three social workers. The configuration of participants for any particular client varies

---

[3] See *EPAS* EP 2.1.3 ("Apply critical thinking to inform and communicate professional judgments").
[4] See *EPAS* EP 2.1.2 ("Apply social work ethical principles to guide professional practice").

dramatically as only one professional per discipline is involved with each case. During the treatment conference, participants share their findings and prepare a treatment plan. For children like Timmy, who require ongoing treatment and therapy, an annual treatment conference is automatically scheduled. Only those professionals involved in ongoing treatment attend later treatment conferences. For instance, a speech therapist would no longer be involved with the case if the child did not require speech therapy. Since Timmy has such extensive treatment needs, professionals from all disciplines will be involved in future conferences.

This agency's policy is to exclude parents and clients from treatment conferences. Some agencies invite clients and/or their families to attend such conferences. Other agencies invite clients and/or families to attend only a designated portion of the conference. Some agencies such as the one providing services to Timmy indicate that having clients and other outsiders present interferes with the frank presentation of information about clients and their families. This agency's staff also feel that conference content may be too emotionally stressful for clients and their families to hear.

2. Ethical questions exist regarding the exclusion of clients and their families from treatment conferences. Discuss the following questions:
   a. How does client exclusion relate to self-determination?
   b. To what extent do clients have the right to know about and be involved in their own assessment and intervention planning?
   c. To what extent is exclusion appropriate?
   d. To what extent is exclusion ethical according to the NASW Code of Ethics?
   e. What is your recommendation—exclusion or inclusion? Explain your rationale.

Competencies/Practice Behaviors Exercise 4.3
What Type of Group Is This?

Focus Competencies or Practice Behaviors:
- EP 2.1.5b   Advocate for human rights and social and economic justice
- EP 2.1.5c   Engage in practices that advance social and economic justice
- EP 2.1.7   Apply knowledge of human behavior and the social environment
- EP 2.1.7b   Critique and apply knowledge to understand person and environment
- EP 2.1.8a   Analyze, formulate, and advocate for policies that advance social well-being
- EP 2.1.8b   Collaborate with colleagues and clients for effective policy action
- EP 2.1.9a   Continuously discover, appraise, and attend to changing locales, populations, scientific and technological developments, and emerging societal trends to provide relevant services
- EP 2.1.9b   Provide leadership in promoting sustainable changes in service delivery and practice to improve the quality of social services

- EP 2.1.10h   Initiate actions to achieve organizational goals
- EP 2.1.10k   Negotiate, mediate, and advocate for clients

A.   Brief Description
Scenarios illustrating various types of groups are read to the class. You are asked to identify what type of group each scenario represents and why.

B.   Objectives
You will:
1.   Assess a variety of task group scenarios.
2.   Discuss what makes various types of task groups unique.
3.   "Critique and apply knowledge [about task groups] to understand person and environment."[5]

C.   Procedure
1.   Review the material on task groups.
2.   Each of the following vignettes will be read. For each, you will be asked what type of group the vignette describes and what aspects about the group helped you to come to that conclusion.

D.   Instructions for Students
1.   Read the following group scenarios, identify what type of group they represent, and indicate what aspects of the group helped you to determine what type of group it was. Types of task groups include: *teams; treatment conferences; administrative groups; delegate councils; committees; and social action groups.*

a.	Chandra, the supervisor of a hospital social work unit, is a member of a group comprised of the hospital director, the head nursing supervisor, and the physical therapy supervisor. Their purpose is to evaluate the hospital's policies regarding job expectations for members of each professional group and make recommendations for changes.

This group is an example of a(n) _____.
What aspects of the group helped you to determine what type of group it was?

---

[5] See *EPAS* EP 2.1.7.

b.   George, a social worker at a group home for adults with chronic mental disorders,[6] is leading a one-time group meeting on behalf of Harry, one of the group home's residents. George is responsible for calling together the home care supervisor, psychiatrist, and daytime care counselors to discuss Harry's case. George will formulate an agenda for the meeting, lead the discussion, solicit feedback from participants, assist the group in establishing intervention plans, and write up the final report including recommendations.

This group is an example of a(n) _____.
What aspects of the group helped you to determine what type of group it was?

c.   Alphonso, a school social worker, was elected by the other workers in his school district to serve as a representative to the state's School Social Work Advocacy Association. This group meets in the state capitol four times each year to identify common issues, discuss concerns, and make recommendations to state legislators that advocate for school policy improvements.

This group is an example of a(n) _____.
What aspects of the group helped you to determine what type of group it was?

d.   Grace, a school social worker at a large residential facility for people with cognitive disabilities, is a member of the agency's Facilities Improvement Group. The group includes representatives from various other agency units such as adult care counselors and educational specialists. The group's task is to evaluate the adequacy of living conditions for residents. Plans include assessment of various institutional facets including: furniture and paint conditions throughout the institution; food preparation and quality; transportation availability for residents (for example, to meet health care and recreational needs); regularity of treatment plan updates; and general staff conduct toward residents. Ultimately, the group will make recommendations to the agency's administration for improvements.

---

[6] Mental disorder or mental illness is "impaired psychosocial or cognitive functioning due to disturbances in any one or more of the following processes: biological, chemical, physiological, genetic, psychological, or social" (Barker, 2003, p. 269). The term "chronic" refers to "problems, abnormal behaviors, and medical conditions that have developed and persisted over a long period" (Barker, 2003, p. 71).

This group is an example of a(n)_____.
What aspects of the group helped you to determine what type of group it was?

---

e. | Suzie is the social worker at a homeless shelter. There she belongs to an internal agency group that include a physician, nurse, psychologist, in-house living supervisor, and vocational counselor. Together, the group works with incoming homeless families, conducting individual and family assessments. Their initial plans involve meeting families' immediate health and survival needs. Long-term planning focuses on permanent housing, access to health care, vocational planning, and counseling needs. They work collaboratively and interdependently to conduct assessments, and to develop and implement treatment plans. Suzie's been working with the group for almost six years now. She thinks they function together pretty well as they're used to each other's little personality quirks.

This group is an example of a(n) _____.
What aspects of the group helped you to determine what type of group it was?

---

f. | Juji, a social worker at a county social services department, organized a group of neighborhood center residents to seek support for a summer sports and recreation program for community youth. The group's goal is to persuade elected county officials who have relevant power to divert some funds to the center so that volunteers might develop and run the program.

This group is an example of a(n) _____.
What aspects of the group helped you to determine what type of group it was?

Competencies/Practice Behaviors Exercise 4.4
Role Play—Observing Group Dynamics in a Social Action Group

Focus Competencies or Practice Behaviors:
- EP 2.1.1a   Advocate for client access to the services of social work
- EP 2.1.3c   Demonstrate effective oral and written communication in working with individuals, families, groups, organizations, communities, and colleagues
- EP 2.1.4   Engage diversity and difference in practice
- EP 2.1.4a   Recognize the extent to which a culture's structures and values may oppress, marginalize, alienate, or create or enhance privilege and power

- EP 2.1.4c   Recognize and communicate their understanding of the importance of difference in shaping life experiences
- EP 2.1.5b   Advocate for human rights and social and economic justice
- EP 2.1.5c   Engage in practices that advance social and economic justice
- EP 2.1.7   Apply knowledge of human behavior and the social environment
- EP 2.1.7b   Critique and apply knowledge to understand person and environment
- EP 2.1.8a   Analyze, formulate, and advocate for policies that advance social well-being
- EP 2.1.8b   Collaborate with colleagues and clients for effective policy action
- EP 2.1.9a   Continuously discover, appraise, and attend to changing locales, populations, scientific and technological developments, and emerging societal trends to provide relevant services
- EP 2.1.9b   Provide leadership in promoting sustainable changes in service delivery and practice to improve the quality of social services
- EP 2.1.10a   Substantively and affectively prepare for action with individuals, families, groups, organizations, and communities
- EP 2.1.10b   Use empathy and other interpersonal skills
- EP 2.1.10c   Develop a mutually agreed-on focus of work and desired outcomes
- EP 2.1.10f   Develop mutually agreed-on intervention goals and objectives
- EP 2.1.10g   Select appropriate intervention strategies
- EP 2.1.10h   Initiate actions to achieve organizational goals
- EP 2.1.10i   Implement prevention interventions that enhance client capacities
- EP 2.1.10j   Help clients resolve problems
- EP 2.1.10k   Negotiate, mediate, and advocate for clients

A.   **Brief Description**

Volunteers role play nine roles in a social action group context while the remainder of the class observes. Ensuing discussion focuses on group dynamics within task groups.

B.   **Objectives**

You will:

1.   Dramatize a simulated task group.
2.   Appraise group interaction within a task group context.
3.   Observe or participate in a simulation designed to "develop a mutually agreed-on focus of work and desired outcomes".[7]
4.   "Critique and apply knowledge [of group dynamics and task groups, specifically, social action groups] to understand person and environment."[8]
5.   Examine the significance of personal hidden agendas.

---

[7] See *EPAS* EP 2.1.10(a) ("Engagement").
[8] See *EPAS* EP 2.1.7.

C. Procedure

1. Review content on group dynamics (see chapter 3) and social action groups.

2. This exercise will be read and you will need to read the content under "D. Instructions for Students." In addition, each role player except for the two playing social workers will receive a "hidden agenda" which will be known only to them.

3. Nine student volunteers will be asked to role play the characters. If no one volunteers, random assignments will be made. Each character's name will be on one side of an 8"x5" notecard bent in half. Each role player will be given her or his hidden agenda and asked not to share its contents with others.

4. The role play will last for 15 to 20 minutes, after which the class will discuss the group dynamics including communication, interpersonal interaction, norms, roles, group cohesion, power and status, and leadership within the group.

D. Instructions for Students

1. Nine volunteers will role play the following roles in a social action group context while the remainder of the class observes. You should you're your respective roles to the best of your ability. Role players have the discretion to play the role beyond its basic description however they see fit.

The Setting

Two Bottleneck County Social Services social workers have become extremely concerned about the large number of women they have encountered lately who complain they have been sexually assaulted. There is no rape crisis center available in the community or at the community's university. The workers decide to see what they might be able to do about it. They call a meeting inviting a number of people in the community who might provide support. The goal is to discuss people's ideas and determine who, if anyone, is willing to start developing a plan. Participants include the following:

Group Facilitators:

Debbie Dogood and Sally Savetheworld (County Social Services Social Workers)

Debbie and Sally are family services workers for Bottleneck County. They are responsible for intake, referral, and some counseling. They have been very concerned about the area's rape problem. They have talked to various professionals, local citizens, and students who concur that it is a serious concern. (Social workers have no hidden agendas. They just want to do something about the problem.)

Below are some suggestions for group facilitation. They may be used either by the two social workers who called the meeting or by other participants who emerge as leaders.

Suggestions for Group Facilitation:
Suggested Techniques

Ask each participant what he/she thinks the problem is.
Ask the physician and cop for suggestions in view of their **expertise**.
Ask the business people and other involved citizens about **possible financial resources**.
You might consider:
- Where do other rape crisis centers get their funding?
- How are such centers structured?
- Are there local/state/federal funds available?
- Who of those participating at the meeting might be able to find out the answers to these questions?
- Should the program focus on helping rape survivors or on rape prevention?

Possible Goals
Possible goals for this meeting (small ones are fine) include:
1. Develop a problem **consensus**.
2. **Make recommendations** for who should do what (for example, who will look for financial resources?).
3. **Set another meeting time.**

Possible Services
Possible types of services to be used or developed might include:
1. A whole new program can be started.
2. An existing program can provide service (for example, the Student Health Center, a local hospital, the police department, county social services department, student counseling center, local churches).
3. An existing program can add on rape crisis counseling as part of its regular services.

Group Participants' Roles

Mrs. Thelma Prissypuff
Mrs. Prissypuff is an upstanding citizen who has lived in Whitewater all her life. She is involved in many volunteer community activities and services. She is married to a successful lawyer who also happens to be President of the local Walrus Lodge.

Dr. Avid Feminist

Dr. Feminist is a University professor and chairperson of the Women's Issues Committee at the university. She is sincerely dedicated to women's issues and to improving the status of women. She is very active in the University's Women's Studies program. She has been a professor at the University for 14 years.

Mr. (Ms.) Robert(a) Filthyrich

Mr. (Ms.) Filthyrich is the local bank president. S/he is a wealthy, well-respected, upstanding pillar of the community. S/he has a history of interest and involvement in supporting worthwhile local services.

Dr. I. M. Superhealer

Dr. Superhealer is a physician with a local practice. She also works part-time at the university Student Health Center. She has a history of interest in women's issues and of participation in community activities for the benefit of women.

Officer Dudley Donowrong

Officer Donowrong is a local police officer. He has dealt with numerous rape victims in the community. He feels rape is a serious problem that needs to be addressed. He is interested in helping if he can.

Ms. Fannie Fettenbacher

Ms. Fettenbacher is the owner of a local business, Fanny's Feminine and Modern Dress Shop. She has owned and run this business for 20 years. She is well known and respected in the community. She is also fairly well off financially. Her husband is deceased. She is interested in the well-being of community women.

Susie Socialworker

Susie is President of the university's Social Work Student Organization. She is very concerned about the rape problem both on campus and in the surrounding community. She would like to help address the problem.

2. After 15 to 20 minutes your instructor will halt the role play for a full-class discussion including the role players' feelings and impressions. The class should address the following issues:

   a. What were the group members' *hidden agendas*?

   b. What was *communication* like within the group? Comment on verbal and nonverbal communication of individual group members.

c. Describe the *interpersonal interaction* within the group. Did specific group members demonstrate mutual respect, liking, disliking, resentment, admiration, encouragement, discouragement, approval, disapproval, or mistrust? If so, who displayed such interaction to whom?

d. What group *norms,* if any, emerged?

e. What *roles* did group members assume and how did they go about doing so?

f. To what extent did the entire group or subsystems of the group manifest *group cohesion*?

g. How did *power and status* develop within the group?

h. Who emerged as *leaders* within the group and how did they accomplish this?

REFERENCES

Barker, R. L. (2003). *The social work dictionary* (5th ed.). Washington, DC: NASW Press.

Council on Social Work Education (CSWE). (2008*). Educational policy and accreditation standards (EPAS).* Alexandria, VA: Author. (Available at www.cswe.org.)

Dubrin, A. J. (2012). Essentials of management (9th ed.). Mason, OH: South-Western.Mish, F. C. (2008). *Merriam-Webster's collegiate dictionary* (11th ed.). Springfield, MA: Merriam-Webster, Incorporated.

Toseland, R. W., & Rivas, R. F. (2012). *An introduction to group work practice* (7th ed.). Boston: Allyn & Bacon.

Chapter 4 Competencies/Practice Behaviors Exercises Assessment:

Name: _____ Date: _____

Supervisor's Name: _____

Focus Competencies/Practice Behaviors:

- EP 2.1.1a   Advocate for client access to the services of social work
- EP 2.1.2   Apply social work ethical principles to guide professional practice
- EP 2.1.2b   Make ethical decisions by applying standards of the National Association of Social Workers Code of Ethics and, as applicable, of the International Federation of Social Workers/International Association of Schools of Social Work Ethics in Social Work, Statement of Principles
- EP 2.1.3   Apply critical thinking to inform and communicate professional judgments
- EP 2.1.3a   Distinguish, appraise, and integrate multiple sources of knowledge, including research-based knowledge and practice wisdom
- EP 2.1.3c   Demonstrate effective oral and written communication in working with individuals, families, groups, organizations, communities, and colleagues
- EP 2.1.4   Engage diversity and difference in practice
- EP 2.1.4a   Recognize the extent to which a culture's structures and values may oppress, marginalize, alienate, or create or enhance privilege and power
- EP 2.1.4c   Recognize and communicate their understanding of the importance of difference in shaping life experiences
- EP 2.1.5b   Advocate for human rights and social and economic justice
- EP 2.1.5c   Engage in practices that advance social and economic justice
- EP 2.1.7   Apply knowledge of human behavior and the social environment
- EP 2.1.7b   Critique and apply knowledge to understand person and environment
- EP 2.1.8a   Analyze, formulate, and advocate for policies that advance social well-being
- EP 2.1.8b   Collaborate with colleagues and clients for effective policy action
- EP 2.1.9a   Continuously discover, appraise, and attend to changing locales, populations, scientific and technological developments, and emerging societal trends to provide relevant services
- EP 2.1.9b   Provide leadership in promoting sustainable changes in service delivery and practice to improve the quality of social services
- EP 2.1.10a   Substantively and affectively prepare for action with individuals, families, groups, organizations, and communities
- EP 2.1.10b   Use empathy and other interpersonal skills
- EP 2.1.10c   Develop a mutually agreed-on focus of work and desired outcomes
- EP 2.1.10f   Develop mutually agreed-on intervention goals and objectives
- EP 2.1.10g   Select appropriate intervention strategies
- EP 2.1.10h   Initiate actions to achieve organizational goals

- EP 2.1.10i   Implement prevention interventions that enhance client capacities
- EP 2.1.10j   Help clients resolve problems
- EP 2.1.10k   Negotiate, mediate, and advocate for clients

Instructions:

A.   Evaluate your work or your partner's work in the Focus Competencies/Practice Behaviors by completing the Competencies/Practice Behaviors Assessment form below

B.   What other Competencies/Practice Behaviors did you use to complete these Exercises? Be sure to record them in your assessments

1.	I have attained this competency/practice behavior (in the range of 81 to 100%)
2.	I have largely attained this competency/practice behavior (in the range of 61 to 80%)
3.	I have partially attained this competency/practice behavior (in the range of 41 to 60%)
4.	I have made a little progress in attaining this competency/practice behavior (in the range of 21 to 40%)
5.	I have made almost no progress in attaining this competency/practice behavior (in the range of 0 to 20%)

EPAS 2008 Core Competencies & Core Practice Behaviors							Student Self Assessment	Evaluator Feedback
Student and Evaluator Assessment Scale and Comments	0	1	2	3	4	5		Agree/Disagree /Comments
EP 2.1.1 Identify as a Professional Social Worker and Conduct Oneself Accordingly:								
a. Advocate for client access to the services of social work								
b. Practice personal reflection and self-correction to assure continual professional development								
c. Attend to professional roles and boundaries								
d. Demonstrate professional demeanor in behavior, appearance, and communication								
e. Engage in career-long learning								
f. Use supervision and consultation								
EP 2.1.2 Apply Social Work Ethical Principles to Guide Professional Practice:								
a. Recognize and manage personal values in a way that allows professional values to guide practice								
b. Make ethical decisions by applying NASW Code of Ethics and, as applicable, of the IFSW/IASSW Ethics in Social Work, Statement of Principles								
c. Tolerate ambiguity in resolving ethical conflicts								
d. Apply strategies of ethical reasoning to arrive at principled decisions								

EP 2.1.3 Apply Critical Thinking to Inform and Communicate Professional Judgments:							
a. Distinguish, appraise, and integrate multiple sources of knowledge, including research-based knowledge and practice wisdom							
b. Analyze models of assessment, prevention, intervention, and evaluation							
c. Demonstrate effective oral and written communication in working with individuals, families, groups, organizations, communities, and colleagues							
EP 2.1.4 Engage Diversity and Difference in Practice:							
a. Recognize the extent to which a culture's structures and values may oppress, marginalize, alienate, or create or enhance privilege and power							
b. Gain sufficient self-awareness to eliminate the influence of personal biases and values in working with diverse groups							
c. Recognize and communicate their understanding of the importance of difference in shaping life experiences							
d. View themselves as learners and engage those with whom they work as informants							
EP 2.1.5 Advance Human Rights and Social and Economic Justice:							
a. Understand forms and mechanisms of oppression and discrimination							
b. Advocate for human rights and social and economic justice							
c. Engage in practices that advance social and economic justice							
EP 2.1.6 Engage in Research-Informed Practice and Practice-Informed Research:							
a. Use practice experience to inform scientific inquiry							
b. Use research evidence to inform practice							
EP 2.1.7 Apply Knowledge of Human Behavior and the Social Environment:							
a. Utilize conceptual frameworks to guide the processes of assessment, intervention, and evaluation							
b. Critique and apply knowledge to understand person and environment							
EP 2.1.8 Engage in Policy Practice to Advance Social and Economic Well-Being and to Deliver Effective Social Work Services:							
a. Analyze, formulate, and advocate for policies that advance social well-being							
b. Collaborate with colleagues and clients for effective policy action							
EP 2.1.9 Respond to Contexts that Shape Practice:							
a. Continuously discover, appraise, and attend to changing locales, populations, scientific and technological developments, and emerging societal trends to provide relevant services							
b. Provide leadership in promoting sustainable changes in service delivery and practice to improve the quality of social services							

EP 2.1.10 Engage, Assess, Intervene, and Evaluate with Individuals, Families, Groups, Organizations and Communities:								
a.	Substantively and affectively prepare for action with individuals, families, groups, organizations, and communities							
b.	Use empathy and other interpersonal skills							
c.	Develop a mutually agreed-on focus of work and desired outcomes							
d.	Collect, organize, and interpret client data							
e.	Assess client strengths and limitations							
f.	Develop mutually agreed-on intervention goals and objectives							
g.	Select appropriate intervention strategies							
h.	Initiate actions to achieve organizational goals							
i.	Implement prevention interventions that enhance client capacities							
j.	Help clients resolve problems							
k.	Negotiate, mediate, and advocate for clients							
l.	Facilitate transitions and endings							
m.	Critically analyze, monitor, and evaluate interventions							

Chapter 5
Knowledge and Theories about Organizations

Competencies/Practice Behaviors Exercise 5.1
Identifying Agency Types

Focus Competencies or Practice Behaviors:
- EP 2.1.7   Apply knowledge of human behavior and the social environment
- EP 2.1.7b   Critique and apply knowledge to understand person and environment
- EP 2.1.10a   Substantively and affectively prepare for action with individuals, families, groups, organizations, and communities

A.   **Brief Description**
You will match types of social services with their respective definitions.

B.   **Objectives**
You will:
1.   Identify various types of social services.
2.   Examine similarities and differences among the various types to explore "the ways social [services] systems promote or deter people in maintaining or achieving health and well-being."[1]

C.   **Procedure**
1.   You will be provided with copies of the matching exercise under "Instructions for Students."
2.   You will be allowed a few minutes to complete the exercise, after which a discussion with the class will be initiated regarding major similarities and differences among these types of social services.

D.   **Instructions for Students**
Match the following terms with their respective definitions provided below:
1.   Social services.................... _____
2.   Institutional services........... _____
3.   Personal social services…... _____
4.   Social agency..................…. _____
5.   Public social agency........... _____
6.   Private social agency.......... _____
7.   Nonprofit social agency…... _____
8.   Proprietary agency.............. _____

---

[1] See Council on Social Work Education (CSWE) *Educational Policy and Accreditation Standards (EPAS) Educational Policy* (EP) 2.1.7, ("Apply knowledge of human behavior and the social environment").

a.   A social services organization that provides some designated social services, often quite similar to those provided by private social agencies, but with the additional aim of making a profit for its owners.

b.   An organization providing social services that typically employs a range of helping professionals including social workers in addition to office staff, paraprofessionals (persons trained to assist professionals), and sometimes volunteers.

c.   Tasks that social work practitioners and other helping professionals perform with the goal of improving people's health, enhancing their quality of life, increasing autonomy and independence, supporting families, and helping people and larger systems improve their functioning in the social environment.

d.   An organization generally providing some type of personal social services that is run to accomplish some service provision goal, not to make financial profit for private owners.

e.   Services that address more individualized needs involving interpersonal relationships and people's ability to function within their immediate environments.

f.   Services provided by major public service systems that administer such benefits as financial assistance, housing programs, health care, or education.

g.   An organization that is privately owned and run by people not employed by government.

h.   An organization run by some designated unit of government and are usually regulated by laws impacting policy.

Competencies/Practice Behaviors Exercise 5.2
Relating Concepts to Theory

Focus Competencies or Practice Behaviors:
- EP 2.1.7a   Utilize conceptual frameworks to guide the processes of assessment, intervention, and evaluation
- EP 2.1.7b   Critique and apply knowledge to understand person and environment

A.   Brief Description
You will match organizational theories with major concepts. Then you will evaluate the concept's significance and assess the similarities and differences among the theories.

B.   Objectives
You will:
1.   Identify major concepts in prevalent organizational theories and "conceptual frameworks" to guide the process of assessing and understanding organizations.[2]
2.   Evaluate each concept's significance to the theory.
3.   "Critique and apply knowledge to understand person and environment" by assessing similarities and differences among the theories.[3]

C.   Procedure
1.   You will be provided with copies of the matching exercise under "D. Instructions for Students."
2.   You will be allowed a few minutes to complete the exercise, after which a discussion with the class will be initiated based on the following queries:
   a.   Explain why each concept is significant to that theory.
   b.   Assess major similarities and differences among the theories.

D.   Instructions to Students
Match the following concepts with the organizational theories they best portray below.

Organizational theories include:
1.   Classical organizational theories.......... _____
2.   Human relations theories.................. _____
3.   Feminist theories........................... _____
4.   Cultural perspective........................ _____
5.   Political-economy theory................. _____
6.   The institutional perspective.............. _____
7.   Contingency theory........................ _____
8.   Culture-Quality theories................... _____
9.   Ecosystems theories....................... _____

Below are a range of concepts that tend to characterize one of the organizational theories presented above.   For each, identify the organizational theory it characterizes.

a.   *Concept:* Emphasis on interpersonal relationships and respect for each other's rights including use of a gender filter, empowerment, the personal as political, the importance of process, and diversity is strength.

b.   *Concept:* Emphasis on how organizations take resources (input) and process them into some kind of product or service (output), and on how all parts of the organization (subsystems) are interrelated and function together to produce output.

---

[2] See *EPAS* EP 2.1.7.
[3] See *EPAS* EP 2.1.7.

c.　*Concept:*　Specifically designed, formal structure and a consistent, rigid organizational network of employees.

d.　*Concept:*　Assumption "that employees want to feel useful and important, that employees have strong social needs, and that these needs are more important than money in motivating employees" (Griffin & Moorhead, 2010, p. 85).

e.　*Concept:*　Emphasis on the assumption that each organization develops a unique mixture of values, standards, presumptions, and practices about how things should be done that eventually result in predictable performance.

f.　*Concept:*　Emphasis on the idea that each element involved in an organization depends on other elements and that employee behavior is complex; therefore, there is no one generally best way to accomplish tasks or goals.

g.　*Concept:*　Emphasis on organizational adaptation to the external environment, with a focus on responses to rules imposed by social institutions; the organization searches for external legitimacy and support to enhance its potential for survival.

i.　*Concept:*　Emphasis on organizational culture and quality improvement, valuing a "strong set of shared positive values and norms within a corporation … while emphasizing quality, service, high performance, and flexibility" (Vecchio, 2006, p. 12).

j.　*Concept:*　Emphasis on organizational adaptation to the external environment, with a focus on resources, power, and a constant struggle to gain power.

Competencies/Practice Behaviors Exercise 5.3
Which Organizational Theory is Best?

Focus Competencies or Practice Behaviors:
- EP 2.1.3a　Distinguish, appraise, and integrate multiple sources of knowledge, including research-based knowledge and practice wisdom
- EP 2.1.3b　Analyze models of assessment, prevention, intervention, and evaluation
- EP 2.1.7a　Utilize conceptual frameworks to guide the processes of assessment, intervention, and evaluation
- EP 2.1.7b　Critique and apply knowledge to understand person and environment

A.　**Brief Description**
You will compare and contrast ten theoretical perspectives on organizations.

B. Objectives

You will:

1. Recognize the basic concepts inherent in ten "conceptual frameworks" to guide the process of assessing and understanding organizations.[4]

2. "Critique and apply knowledge to understand person and environment" by assessing similarities and differences among the ten approaches.[5]

C. Procedure

1. Review the material on theoretical perspectives on organizations.

2. The class will be divided into small groups of four to six.

3. The groups will discuss the subsequent questions, select a group representative, and be prepared to report to the entire class the small group's findings.

4. After about 20 minutes, the small groups will be asked to terminate their discussions and participate in a full-class discussion.

5. A representative from each group will be asked to share her or his summary of the discussion. Comments from all class members will be encouraged.

D. Instructions for Students

1. Identify the primary concepts involved in each of the following theoretical perspectives on organizations:

    a. Classical organizational theories
    b. Neoclassical organizational theories
    c. Human relations theories
    d. Feminist theories
    e. Cultural perspective
    f. Political-economy theory
    g. The institutional perspective
    h. Contingency theory
    i. Culture-Quality theories
    j. Ecosystems theories

2. Describe the similarities and differences among the above perspectives.

---

[4] See *EPAS* EP 2.1.7.
[5] See *EPAS* EP 2.1.7.

Focus Competencies or Practice Behaviors:
- EP 2.1.2b   Make ethical decisions by applying standards of the National Association of Social Workers Code of Ethics and, as applicable, of the International Federation of Social Workers/International Association of Schools of Social Work Ethics in Social Work, Statement of Principles
- EP 2.1.7a   Utilize conceptual frameworks to guide the processes of assessment, intervention, and evaluation
- EP 2.1.7b   Critique and apply knowledge to understand person and environment

A.   **Brief Description**
In small groups, you will relate professional social work values to six organizational theories.

B.   **Objectives**
You will:
1.   "Apply social work ethical principles" to various organizational theories.[6]
2.   "Critique and apply knowledge [about organizational theories] to understand person and environment."[7]

C.   **Procedure**
1.   Review the content on the *NASW Code of Ethics* six core values (portrayed in Section D below).
2.   The class will be divided into small groups of four to six.
3.   Discuss how each ethical core value relates to each of the six theories.
4.   After approximately 20 minutes, you will participate in a full-class discussion to share each group's findings.

D.   **Instructions for Students**
1.   Your instructor will review the following core values emphasized in the *NASW Code of Ethics* (NASW, 1999):
   a.   *Service:*   Providing help, resources, and benefits so that people may achieve their maximum potential.
   b.   *Social justice:*   Upholding the condition that in a perfect world, all citizens would have identical "rights, protection, opportunities, obligations, and social benefits" regardless of their backgrounds and membership in diverse groups (Barker, 2003, pp. 404-405).
   c.   *Dignity and worth of the person:*   Holding in high esteem and appreciating individual value.

---

[6] See *EPAS* EP 2.1.2 ("Apply social work ethical principles to guide professional practice").
[7] See *EPAS* EP 2.1.7.

d.   *Importance of human relationships:*   Valuing the dynamic reciprocal interactions between social workers and clients, including how they communicate, think and feel about each other, and behave toward each other.

e.   *Integrity:*   Maintaining trustworthiness and sound adherence to moral ideals.

f.   *Competence:*   Having the necessary skills and abilities to perform work with clients effectively.

2.   In small groups and address the following question:
To what extent do each of the following theories comply with the six core professional values?
- Classical organizational theories
- Human relations theories
- Feminist theories
- The cultural perspective
- The institutional perspective
- Contingency theory

3.   Be prepared to share your conclusions with the entire class during a subsequent full-class discussion.

REFERENCES

Barker, R. L. (2003). *The social work dictionary* (5th ed.). Washington, DC: NASW Press.

Council on Social Work Education (CSWE). (2008). *Educational policy and accreditation standards (EPAS).* Alexandria, VA: Author. (Available at www.cswe.org.)

Griffin, R. W., & Moorhead, G. (2010). *Organizational behavior: Managing people and organizations* (9th ed.). Mason, OH: South-Western.

National Association of Social Workers (NASW). (1999). *NASW code of ethics* (amended). Washington, DC: Author.

Vecchio, R. P. (2006). *Organizational behavior* (6th ed.). Mason, OH: South-Western.

Chapter 5 Competencies/Practice Behaviors Exercises Assessment:

Name: _____   **Date:** _____

Supervisor's Name: _____

Focus Competencies/Practice Behaviors:

- EP 2.1.2b   Make ethical decisions by applying standards of the National Association of Social Workers Code of Ethics and, as applicable, of the International Federation of Social Workers/International Association of Schools of Social Work Ethics in Social Work, Statement of Principles
- EP 2.1.3a   Distinguish, appraise, and integrate multiple sources of knowledge, including research-based knowledge and practice wisdom
- EP 2.1.3b   Analyze models of assessment, prevention, intervention, and evaluation
- EP 2.1.7   Apply knowledge of human behavior and the social environment
- EP 2.1.7a   Utilize conceptual frameworks to guide the processes of assessment, intervention, and evaluation
- EP 2.1.7b   Critique and apply knowledge to understand person and environment
- EP 2.1.10a   Substantively and affectively prepare for action with individuals, families, groups, organizations, and communities

Instructions:

A.   Evaluate your work or your partner's work in the Focus Competencies/Practice Behaviors by completing the Competencies/Practice Behaviors Assessment form below

B.   What other Competencies/Practice Behaviors did you use to complete these Exercises? Be sure to record them in your assessments

1.	I have attained this competency/practice behavior (in the range of 81 to 100%)
2.	I have largely attained this competency/practice behavior (in the range of 61 to 80%)
3.	I have partially attained this competency/practice behavior (in the range of 41 to 60%)
4.	I have made a little progress in attaining this competency/practice behavior (in the range of 21 to 40%)
5.	I have made almost no progress in attaining this competency/practice behavior (in the range of 0 to 20%)

EPAS 2008 Core Competencies & Core Practice Behaviors	Student Self Assessment						Evaluator Feedback
Student and Evaluator Assessment Scale and Comments	0	1	2	3	4	5	Agree/Disagree /Comments
EP 2.1.1 Identify as a Professional Social Worker and Conduct Oneself Accordingly:							
a. Advocate for client access to the services of social work							
b. Practice personal reflection and self-correction to assure continual professional development							
c. Attend to professional roles and boundaries							
d. Demonstrate professional demeanor in behavior, appearance, and communication							
e. Engage in career-long learning							
f. Use supervision and consultation							
EP 2.1.2 Apply Social Work Ethical Principles to Guide Professional Practice:							
a. Recognize and manage personal values in a way that allows professional values to guide practice							
b. Make ethical decisions by applying NASW Code of Ethics and, as applicable, of the IFSW/IASSW Ethics in Social Work, Statement of Principles							
c. Tolerate ambiguity in resolving ethical conflicts							
d. Apply strategies of ethical reasoning to arrive at principled decisions							
EP 2.1.3 Apply Critical Thinking to Inform and Communicate Professional Judgments:							
a. Distinguish, appraise, and integrate multiple sources of knowledge, including research-based knowledge and practice wisdom							
b. Analyze models of assessment, prevention, intervention, and evaluation							
c. Demonstrate effective oral and written communication in working with individuals, families, groups, organizations, communities, and colleagues							
EP 2.1.4 Engage Diversity and Difference in Practice:							
a. Recognize the extent to which a culture's structures and values may oppress, marginalize, alienate, or create or enhance privilege and power							
b. Gain sufficient self-awareness to eliminate the influence of personal biases and values in working with diverse groups							
c. Recognize and communicate their understanding of the importance of difference in shaping life experiences							
d. View themselves as learners and engage those with whom they work as informants							
EP 2.1.5 Advance Human Rights and Social and Economic Justice:							
a. Understand forms and mechanisms of oppression and discrimination							
b. Advocate for human rights and social and economic justice							
c. Engage in practices that advance social and economic justice							

EP 2.1.6 Engage in Research-Informed Practice and Practice-Informed Research:							
a. Use practice experience to inform scientific inquiry							
b. Use research evidence to inform practice							
EP 2.1.7 Apply Knowledge of Human Behavior and the Social Environment:							
a. Utilize conceptual frameworks to guide the processes of assessment, intervention, and evaluation							
b. Critique and apply knowledge to understand person and environment							
EP 2.1.8 Engage in Policy Practice to Advance Social and Economic Well-Being and to Deliver Effective Social Work Services:							
a. Analyze, formulate, and advocate for policies that advance social well-being							
b. Collaborate with colleagues and clients for effective policy action							
EP 2.1.9 Respond to Contexts that Shape Practice:							
a. Continuously discover, appraise, and attend to changing locales, populations, scientific and technological developments, and emerging societal trends to provide relevant services							
b. Provide leadership in promoting sustainable changes in service delivery and practice to improve the quality of social services							
EP 2.1.10 Engage, Assess, Intervene, and Evaluate with Individuals, Families, Groups, Organizations and Communities:							
a. Substantively and affectively prepare for action with individuals, families, groups, organizations, and communities							
b. Use empathy and other interpersonal skills							
c. Develop a mutually agreed-on focus of work and desired outcomes							
d. Collect, organize, and interpret client data							
e. Assess client strengths and limitations							
f. Develop mutually agreed-on intervention goals and objectives							
g. Select appropriate intervention strategies							
h. Initiate actions to achieve organizational goals							
i. Implement prevention interventions that enhance client capacities							
j. Help clients resolve problems							
k. Negotiate, mediate, and advocate for clients							
l. Facilitate transitions and endings							
m. Critically analyze, monitor, and evaluate interventions							

Chapter 6
Social Service Organizational Settings, Goals, and Environmental Contexts

---

Competencies/Practice Behaviors Exercise 6.1
Understanding Organizational Goals

Focus Competencies or Practice Behaviors:
- EP 2.1.7   Apply knowledge of human behavior and the social environment
- EP 2.1.7b   Critique and apply knowledge to understand person and environment

A.   **Brief Description**
You will match various concepts concerning goals with their respective meanings.

B.   **Objectives**
You will:
1.   "Critique and apply knowledge to understand person and environment" by discussing various concepts involving goals.[1]

C.   **Procedure**
1.   You will be provided with copies of the matching exercise under "D. Instructions for Students."
2.   You will be allowed a few minutes to complete the exercise, followed by a discussion with the class regarding the following questions:
   a.   In what ways are these concepts different?
   b.   In what ways are these concepts similar?
   c.   What are the reasons why organizations have different types of goals?
   d.   To what extent are these different types of goals helpful or harmful in terms of the organization's effective functioning?
   e.   How would organizations ideally function?

D.   **Instructions for Students**
Match the following concepts concerning goals with their respective meanings.

1.	Organizational goal	_____
2.	Official goal	_____
3.	Operational goal	_____
4.	Goal displacement	_____
5.	Mission statement	_____

---

[1] See Council on Social Work Education (CSWE) *Educational Policy and Accreditation Standards (EPAS)* Educational Policy (EP) 2.1.7, ("Apply knowledge of human behavior and the social environment").

a. "Explicit or implicit" objectives that are likely "inferred from actual practices" employees follow within the organization (Lauffer, 2011, p. 27).

b. "Substitution of a legitimate goal with another goal which the organization was not developed to address, for which resources were not allocated and which it is not known to serve" (Etzioni, 1964, p. 10). This often "occurs when an organization moves in different directions from its original purpose" (Netting & O'Connor, 2003, p. 51).

c. A statement "of expected outcomes dealing with the problem that the program is attempting to prevent, eradicate, or ameliorate. They are responsive to problems and needs, and represent an ideal or hoped-for outcome" (Kettner, Moroney, & Martin, 2013, p.131).

d. Stated intentions that "explain agency purposes" and "gather support and legitimacy for agency operations"; "they are often found in such formal documents as agency mission statements, incorporation papers, Web sites, annual reports, and promotional materials" (Lauffer, 2011, p. 27).

e. A declaration of the organization's purpose that "establishes broad and relatively permanent parameters within which goals are developed and specific programs designed" (Kettner et al., 2013, p. 130).

Competencies/Practice Behaviors Exercise 6.2
Critiquing the Internal Organizational Environment

Focus Competencies or Practice Behaviors:

- EP 2.1.4a   Recognize the extent to which a culture's structures and values may oppress, marginalize, alienate, or create or enhance privilege and power
- EP 2.1.5a   Understand forms and mechanisms of oppression and discrimination
- EP 2.1.5c   Engage in practices that advance social and economic justice
- EP 2.1.7   Apply knowledge of human behavior and the social environment
- EP 2.1.7b   Critique and apply knowledge to understand person and environment
- EP 2.1.8a   Analyze, formulate, and advocate for policies that advance social well-being
- EP 2.1.10k   Negotiate, mediate, and advocate for clients

A. Brief Description

In small groups, you identify problems in an internal agency environment, and make suggestions for improvements.

B. **Objectives**
   You will:
   1. "Critique and apply knowledge [of organizational macro systems] to understand person and environment" by identifying and examining problems inherent in an internal agency environment portrayed by a vignette.[2]
   2. Suggest means of improvement.
   3. Evaluate the costs and benefits of suggested improvements.

C. **Procedure**
   1. The vignette below will be read to the entire class.
   2. The class will be divided into small groups of four to six.
   3. The groups will be asked to discuss the questions following the vignette, select a group representative, and be prepared to report to the entire class the small group's findings.
   4. After about 15 minutes, the small groups will be asked to terminate their discussions and participate in a full-class discussion.
   5. A representative from each group will be asked to share her or his summary of the discussion. Comments will be encouraged from all class members.

D. **Instructions for Students**
   1. Read the following scenario and discuss the subsequent questions using a small group format.

> **SCENARIO:** A large county Department of Social Services (previously referred to as "the public welfare department") comes to mind. It is located in the shell of an old department store with high ceilings and a myriad of small worker cubicles somewhat resembling a mammoth beehive. All outside windows have been sealed with bricks because of "the heating and ventilation problems." No one really knows what that means. However, everyone inside the building knows that the building's interior is isolated from the outside world.
>
> When entering the main door of the building, it is extremely difficult to figure out where to go for what kind of services. This is true even if you're a professional social worker, let alone if you're a client entering the building for the first time. Consider what it would be like if you were a client applying for services from this agency. You probably have to stand in line for fifteen or twenty minutes simply to get the information you need to find out where to go.
>
> When you finally wander into a waiting area for the services you need, you have to stand in line again for another twenty minutes or so to get the forms you must fill out for the services you need. You then take the twenty pages of complicated forms, which you fill out meticulously, and take a seat. The chairs are made of hard plastic. There are large "dust bunnies" (sometimes referred to as "dinosaur dust bunnies") rolling around your feet. It then takes approximately an

[2] See *EPAS* EP 2.1.7.

hour to fill out the forms. This is assuming you can read well in English. You probably do not understand some of the questions so you leave the spaces blank. You then take the forms up to the desk where they are placed in a pile. You must wait your turn in order to see an intake worker (that is, someone who begins the process to provide services). You wait two to three hours.

Finally, your name is called and you are instructed to go to Cubicle 57 to see Ms. Hardmoney. You enter Cubicle 57 and see Ms. Hardmoney sitting at her desk and reading your forms. You then begin a discussion with her concerning the additional information she needs in order to process your application for services. It seems, she indicates, that a number of critical elements of information are missing. Look at those blanks. She then says you must get the critical information before you can continue the application process. The critical information is somewhere at home. Well, that's all right. Just go home, get it, and start this whole process over again tomorrow. At least you know where the waiting room is now.

2. Discuss the following questions:
    a. What problems are portrayed in this internal agency environment?
    b. In what ways might the agency have been more responsive to the needs and comforts of clients?
    c. Improvements usually involve higher costs in terms of financial resources and staff time. To what extent do you feel the benefits resulting from your suggestions for improvements merit the costs?

Competencies/Practice Behaviors Exercise 6.3
Evaluating the Effects of TANF

Focus Competencies or Practice Behaviors:
- EP 2.1.3   Apply critical thinking to inform and communicate professional judgments
- EP 2.1.4a   Recognize the extent to which a culture's structures and values may oppress, marginalize, alienate, or create or enhance privilege and power
- EP 2.1.5b   Advocate for human rights and social and economic justice
- EP 2.1.7b   Critique and apply knowledge to understand person and environment
- EP 2.1.8a   Analyze, formulate, and advocate for policies that advance social well-being
- EP 2.1.9a   Continuously discover, appraise, and attend to changing locales, populations, scientific and technological developments, and emerging societal trends to provide relevant services

A. **Brief Description**
    The class is broken down into small groups and asked to evaluate the effects of Temporary Assistance to Needy Families (TANF) by discussing a case scenario.

B. **Objectives**
You will:
1. Explore "the ways social systems [i.e., organizational macro systems] promote or deter people in maintaining or achieving health and well-being."[3]
2. Identify some of the pros and cons of TANF.
3. Appraise the potential effects of TANF on poor, single mothers and their families.
4. Propose suggestions for how public assistance policy might be improved.

C. **Procedure**
1. Review the content on TANF.
2. The vignette below will be read to the entire class.
3. The class will be divided into small groups of four to six.
4. The groups will be asked to discuss the questions following the vignette, select a group representative, and be prepared to report to the entire class the small group's findings.
5. After about 15 minutes, the small groups will be asked to terminate their discussions and participate in a full-class discussion.
6. A representative from each group will be asked to share her or his summary of the discussion. Comments will be encouraged from all class members.

D. **Instructions for Students**
1. Read the following case example and address the subsequent questions.

> *CASE EXAMPLE:* Kaitlyn, 24, is a single mother with three children Sean, 2, Shane, 4, and Shannon, 5. She has an eleventh grade education, as she dropped out of high school to live with Irving, the children's father. Irving, 35, had lived with the family for six years until one year ago when he abruptly left without warning. Kaitlyn thought she had been smelling a woman's perfume on his clothing for several months prior to his leaving. Although Kaitlyn loved Irving, he had refused to marry her, maintaining that marriage only ruins the spontaneity in a relationship. One Sunday Kaitlyn came home from visiting her mother and abruptly discovered that Irving had left with all his things—along with the TV, the DVR, the MP3 player, the blender, her crock pot, and some jewelry she had inherited from an aunt. At that point she wished she would have gone through with cutting every third stitch out of the seams holding his trousers together, a plan she had earlier considered after suspecting his infidelity.
>
> Kaitlyn thought she and Irving had been happy. Now Irving is nowhere to be found. His work history involved a series of briefly held, part-time unskilled jobs. He has no immediate relatives. She feels he would be virtually impossible to track down.

---

[3] See *EPAS* EP 2.1.7.

For the past year since Irving disappeared, Kaitlyn was forced to apply for public assistance and compelled to undergo some job training aimed at placement in a food service setting. She had recently gotten a minimum wage job for 35 hours a week as a cook at Boogie's Burger Heaven. The job would be subsidized by state TANF funds for the next year. (The intent of such subsidy is to encourage businesses to hire TANF recipients, as what actually came out of the business' pockets to pay employees is considerably less than minimum wage.) Boogie's does not provide health insurance for its employees.

Kaitlyn enjoys her work and her fellow employees. She feels proud of getting back on her feet again and becoming independent. However, there are a few issues about which she has nagging concerns.

First she has to work a lot of nights. Her children attend a publicly funded daycare center, but it closes at 8:00 p.m. Sometimes, she's scheduled to work two nights a week until midnight. She then must impose on her neighbors or her mother to baby-sit. Her mother has arthritis and chronic bronchial problems so finds it difficult to help out.

A second issue is that Shannon finds daycare really boring and is beginning to manifest some behavioral problems when she's there. Daycare staff have started to threaten Kaitlyn that if Shannon doesn't "shape up," they'll expel her.

A third concern is that Shane has been diagnosed with Tourette's syndrome, "a neurological disorder beginning in childhood ... in which stereotyped motor movements (tics) are accompanied by multiple vocal outbursts that may include grunting or barking noises or socially inappropriate words or statements" (Hallahan & Kauffman, 2006, p. 256). Although daycare staff and babysitting neighbors tend to like Shane and tolerate his increasingly inappropriate and uncontrollable behavior, Kaitlyn thinks they're beginning to tire of it. Meanwhile, Kaitlyn is working with medical specialists to administer, monitor, and adapt medications to help control Shane's tics and outbursts. She has been told this will be a lifelong process.

A fourth issue is that Sean is not yet toilet trained. Kaitlyn finds it impossible to maintain consistency when she is at work so often and he is in the care of so many different people.

Finally, although Kaitlyn likes her job, she aspires to something that would provide her with a better future. She would like to get her GED (general education development, general education diploma, or high school equivalency). Ideally, she would prefer to work in a professional office, perhaps as an optometrist's assistant or doing something with computers.

2.   Discuss the following questions:
    a.   In what ways is TANF helping Kaitlyn and her family survive?
    b.   In what ways is TANF limiting Kaitlyn's ability to attain her and her family's optimal health and well-being?

c.   What do you see as Kaitlyn's future problems in view of TANF's restrictions?

d.   In what ways might public assistance help Kaitlyn become more independent and improve her and her family's health, well-being, and quality of life?

REFERENCES

Council on Social Work Education (CSWE). (2008). *Educational policy and accreditation standards (EPAS)*. Alexandria, VA: Author. (Available at www.cswe.org.)

Etzioni, A. (1964). *Modern organizations*. Englewood Cliffs, NJ: Prentice-Hall.

Hallahan, D. P., & Kauffman, J. M. (2006). *Exceptional children* (10th ed.). Boston: Allyn & Bacon.

Kettner, P. M., Moroney, R. M., & Martin, L. L. (2013). *Designing and managing programs: An effectiveness-based approach* (4th ed.). Thousand Oaks, CA: Sage.

Lauffer, A. (2011). *Understanding your social agency* (3rd ed.). Thousand Oaks, CA: Sage.

Netting, F. E. & O'Connor, M. K. (2003). *Organization practice: A social worker's guide to understanding human services*. Boston: Allyn & Bacon.

Chapter 6 Competencies/Practice Behaviors Exercises Assessment:

Name: _____ Date: _____

Supervisor's Name: _____

Focus Competencies/Practice Behaviors:

- EP 2.1.3   Apply critical thinking to inform and communicate professional judgments
- EP 2.1.4a   Recognize the extent to which a culture's structures and values may oppress, marginalize, alienate, or create or enhance privilege and power
- EP 2.1.5a   Understand forms and mechanisms of oppression and discrimination
- EP 2.1.5b   Advocate for human rights and social and economic justice
- EP 2.1.5c   Engage in practices that advance social and economic justice
- EP 2.1.7   Apply knowledge of human behavior and the social environment
- EP 2.1.7b   Critique and apply knowledge to understand person and environment
- EP 2.1.8a   Analyze, formulate, and advocate for policies that advance social well-being
- EP 2.1.9a   Continuously discover, appraise, and attend to changing locales, populations, scientific and technological developments, and emerging societal trends to provide relevant services
- EP 2.1.10k   Negotiate, mediate, and advocate for clients

Instructions:

A.   Evaluate your work or your partner's work in the Focus Competencies/Practice Behaviors by completing the Competencies/Practice Behaviors Assessment form below

B.   What other Competencies/Practice Behaviors did you use to complete these Exercises? Be sure to record them in your assessments

1.	I have attained this competency/practice behavior (in the range of 81 to 100%)
2.	I have largely attained this competency/practice behavior (in the range of 61 to 80%)
3.	I have partially attained this competency/practice behavior (in the range of 41 to 60%)
4.	I have made a little progress in attaining this competency/practice behavior (in the range of 21 to 40%)
5.	I have made almost no progress in attaining this competency/practice behavior (in the range of 0 to 20%)

EPAS 2008 Core Competencies & Core Practice Behaviors			Student Self Assessment					Evaluator Feedback	
Student and Evaluator Assessment Scale and Comments	0	1	2	3	4	5	Agree/Disagree /Comments		
EP 2.1.1 Identify as a Professional Social Worker and Conduct Oneself Accordingly:									
a. Advocate for client access to the services of social work									
b. Practice personal reflection and self-correction to assure continual professional development									
c. Attend to professional roles and boundaries									
d. Demonstrate professional demeanor in behavior, appearance, and communication									
e. Engage in career-long learning									
f. Use supervision and consultation									
EP 2.1.2 Apply Social Work Ethical Principles to Guide Professional Practice:									
a. Recognize and manage personal values in a way that allows professional values to guide practice									
b. Make ethical decisions by applying NASW Code of Ethics and, as applicable, of the IFSW/IASSW Ethics in Social Work, Statement of Principles									
c. Tolerate ambiguity in resolving ethical conflicts									
d. Apply strategies of ethical reasoning to arrive at principled decisions									
EP 2.1.3 Apply Critical Thinking to Inform and Communicate Professional Judgments:									
a. Distinguish, appraise, and integrate multiple sources of knowledge, including research-based knowledge and practice wisdom									
b. Analyze models of assessment, prevention, intervention, and evaluation									
c. Demonstrate effective oral and written communication in working with individuals, families, groups, organizations, communities, and colleagues									
EP 2.1.4 Engage Diversity and Difference in Practice:									
a. Recognize the extent to which a culture's structures and values may oppress, marginalize, alienate, or create or enhance privilege and power									
b. Gain sufficient self-awareness to eliminate the influence of personal biases and values in working with diverse groups									
c. Recognize and communicate their understanding of the importance of difference in shaping life experiences									
d. View themselves as learners and engage those with whom they work as informants									
EP 2.1.5 Advance Human Rights and Social and Economic Justice:									
a. Understand forms and mechanisms of oppression and discrimination									
b. Advocate for human rights and social and economic justice									
c. Engage in practices that advance social and economic justice									

EP 2.1.6 Engage in Research-Informed Practice and Practice-Informed Research:							
a. Use practice experience to inform scientific inquiry							
b. Use research evidence to inform practice							
EP 2.1.7 Apply Knowledge of Human Behavior and the Social Environment:							
a. Utilize conceptual frameworks to guide the processes of assessment, intervention, and evaluation							
b. Critique and apply knowledge to understand person and environment							
EP 2.1.8 Engage in Policy Practice to Advance Social and Economic Well-Being and to Deliver Effective Social Work Services:							
a. Analyze, formulate, and advocate for policies that advance social well-being							
b. Collaborate with colleagues and clients for effective policy action							
EP 2.1.9 Respond to Contexts that Shape Practice:							
a. Continuously discover, appraise, and attend to changing locales, populations, scientific and technological developments, and emerging societal trends to provide relevant services							
b. Provide leadership in promoting sustainable changes in service delivery and practice to improve the quality of social services							
EP 2.1.10 Engage, Assess, Intervene, and Evaluate with Individuals, Families, Groups, Organizations and Communities:							
a. Substantively and affectively prepare for action with individuals, families, groups, organizations, and communities							
b. Use empathy and other interpersonal skills							
c. Develop a mutually agreed-on focus of work and desired outcomes							
d. Collect, organize, and interpret client data							
e. Assess client strengths and limitations							
f. Develop mutually agreed-on intervention goals and objectives							
g. Select appropriate intervention strategies							
h. Initiate actions to achieve organizational goals							
i. Implement prevention interventions that enhance client capacities							
j. Help clients resolve problems							
k. Negotiate, mediate, and advocate for clients							
l. Facilitate transitions and endings							
m. Critically analyze, monitor, and evaluate interventions							

Chapter 7
Organizational Structure and Dynamics

Competencies/Practice Behaviors Exercise 7.1
Understanding Internal Organizational Environments

Focus Competencies or Practice Behaviors:
- EP 2.1.7   Apply knowledge of human behavior and the social environment
- EP 2.1.7b   Critique and apply knowledge to understand person and environment
- EP 2.1.10a Substantively and affectively prepare for action with individuals, families, groups, organizations, and communities

A.   **Brief Description**
      You will match various concepts important in understanding human behavior in traditional organizational environments.

B.   **Objectives**
      You will:
      1.   "Apply knowledge of human behavior and the social environment" by identifying basic components involved in five dimensions of agency structure and culture.[1]
      2.   Compare and contrast these dimensions.
      3.   Explain the relevance of each dimension.

C.   **Procedure**
      1.   You will be provided with copies of the matching exercise under "D. Instructions for Students."
      2.   You will be allowed a few minutes to complete the exercise, after which a full-class discussion will be initiated regarding the following questions and issues:
            a.   Identify the key components involved in each of these concepts.
            b.   In what ways are these five concepts different?
            c.   In what ways are these five concepts similar?
            d.   Explain how each concept is important for understanding how organizations function.

---

[1] See Council on Social Work Education (CSWE) *Educational Policy and Accreditation Standards (EPAS)* Educational Policy (EP) 2.1.7, ("Apply knowledge of human behavior and the social environment").

D. **Instructions for Students**

Match the following concepts with their respective meanings.

1. Organizational culture _____
2. Organizational structure _____
3. Lines of authority _____
4. Channels of communication _____
5. Power _____

a. The potential ability to move people on a chosen course to produce an effect or achieve some goal.

b. "The set of key values, beliefs, understandings, and norms shared by members of an organization" involving "a pattern of shared values and assumptions about how things are done within the organization" (Daft & Marcic, 2013, p.70).

c. Numerous, complex systems of verbal and nonverbal exchange whereby staff members convey and receive information.

d. The specific administrative and supervisory responsibilities of supervisors involving their supervisees, often illustrated by an organizational chart.

e. "The system of task, reporting, and authority relationships within which the work of an organization is done" (Griffin & Moorhead, 2012, p. 434).

> **Competencies/Practice Behaviors Exercise 7.2**
> **The Importance of Good Supervision**

Focus Competencies or Practice Behaviors:
- EP 2.1.1   Identify as a professional social worker and conduct oneself accordingly
- EP 2.1.1f   Use supervision and consultation
- EP 2.1.7   Apply knowledge of human behavior and the social environment
- EP 2.1.7b   Critique and apply knowledge to understand person and environment
- EP 2.1.10a Substantively and affectively prepare for action with individuals, families, groups, organizations, and communities

A. **Brief Description**

Using a small group format, you will discuss your experiences in supervision and assess qualities that make supervision effective or ineffective.

B. Objectives

You will:
1. "Apply knowledge of human behavior and the social environment" by analyzing the concept of supervision.[2]
2. Examine "professional conduct and growth" by exploring the use of supervision.[3]

C. Procedure
1. Review the content on supervision.
2. The class will be divided into small groups of four to six.
3. The groups will be asked to discuss the questions posed below in "D. Instructions for Students." Each group should be prepared to summarize its findings in a subsequent full-class discussion.
4. After 10 to 15 minutes, group representatives will be asked to summary their findings for the entire class. Comments will be encouraged from others in class.

D. Instructions for Students
1. Your instructor will divide you up into small groups of four to six.
2. Discuss the following questions:
   a. What types of jobs have you held?
   b. In what types of organizations (e.g., businesses) have you worked?
   c. What were your supervisors like?
   d. Picture one or two of your supervisors in your mind. (For the purposes of this exercise, it's probably best to choose either your best or worst supervisors.) Evaluate each according to the following variables and explain your reasons. To what extent was this specific supervisor:
      - Competent?
      - Supportive of your work?
      - Capable of providing you with help when you needed it?
      - A good communication link between you and upper levels of management or administration?
      - A good facilitator of cooperation among you and other staff?
      - Effective at resolving intra-staff conflicts?
      - A fair and reasonable evaluator of your job performance?
      - Effective at providing you with positive feedback about good performance?
      - Helpful in terms of facilitating the development of new skills?

---

[2] See *EPAS* EP 2.1.7.

[3] See *EPAS* EP 2.1.1 ("Identify as a professional social worker and conduct oneself accordingly").

Focus Competencies or Practice Behaviors:
- EP 2.1.7   Apply knowledge of human behavior and the social environment
- EP 2.1.7b   Critique and apply knowledge to understand person and environment

A.   Brief Description

You will participate in a discussion concerning your college or university's organizational structure, and the extent to which your university, college, and social work program is centralized or decentralized.

B.   Objectives

You will:

1.   "Critique and apply knowledge [of the organizational structure and culture of their university, college, and social work program] to understand person and environment."[4]

2.   Apply knowledge of human behavior concerning the educational macro system with which they're involved.[5]

3.   Appraise the strengths and weaknesses of these aspects of college life.

C.   Procedure

1.   Review the content on organizational culture and structure.

2.   A discussion will be initiated focusing on the questions cited below under "D. Instructions for Students."

D.   Instructions for Students

Address the following questions:

1.   What do you know about your university, college, and social work program's organizational structure and culture?

2.   To what extent is it centralized (that is, run primarily according to classical scientific management theories with clearly established lines of authority and little staff/faculty discretion) or decentralized (allowing for a great deal of staff/faculty discretion)? Explain.

3.   What are the strengths and weaknesses of the organizational structure in your university, college, and social work program?

---

[4] See *EPAS* EP 2.1.7.
[5] See *EPAS* EP 2.1.7.

Focus Competencies or Practice Behaviors:
- EP 2.1.4a   Recognize the extent to which a culture's structures and values may oppress, marginalize, alienate, or create or enhance privilege and power
- EP 2.1.7   Apply knowledge of human behavior and the social environment
- EP 2.1.7b   Critique and apply knowledge to understand person and environment
- EP 2.1.10   Engage, assess, intervene, and evaluate with individuals, families, groups, organizations, and communities

A.   **Brief Description**
You will be given an assignment to interview a staff person at a social services agency, and explore the formal lines of authority, actual channels of communication, power, and politics operating within the organization.

B.   **Objectives**
You will:
1.   "Critique and apply knowledge to understand person and environment" by identifying and examining the formal lines of authority, actual channels of communication, power, and politics operating within an organization.[6]
2.   Compare and contrast the formal and informal organizational structures.

C.   **Procedure**
1.   Review the material on organizational structure.

D.   **Instructions for Students**
Choose an organization, preferably some type of social services agency. For the purposes of this assignment, however, any agency – including your university or some segment of the university – will do. Contact an employee, a supervisor, or an administrator in the agency you selected, and ask for a copy of the organizational chart. Explain to your contact person that you want to study the formal *lines of authority* illustrated in the chart, and contrast them to the actual *channels of communication, power,* and *politics* operating within the organization.
    Define these terms for your contact, then ask the following questions, record your interviewee's answers, and summarize your results in a paper:
1.   To what extent do the channels of communication in the agency follow the formal lines of authority depicted in the organizational chart?
2.   If there are specific differences between the chart and the reality, describe them.
3.   What are the positive and negative effects of these differences?

---

[6] See *EPAS* EP 2.1.7.

4. How closely do the power and politics in the agency match the formal lines of authority depicted in the organizational chart?
5. If there are specific differences between the chart and the reality, describe them.
6. What are the positive and negative effects of these differences?

Competencies/Practice Behaviors Exercise 7.5
People and Power

Focus Competencies or Practice Behaviors:
- EP 2.1.5a   Understand forms and mechanisms of oppression and discrimination
- EP 2.1.10a Substantively and affectively prepare for action with individuals, families, groups, organizations, and communities

A. Brief Description
You will explore the various types of power manifested by a range of people in organizational and political settings.

B. Objectives
You will:
1. "Critique and apply knowledge to understand person and environment" by recognizing the types of power demonstrated by people in visible public positions.[7]
2. Examine the reasons for these sources of power

C. Procedure
1. Review the material on types of power including *legitimate, reward, coercive, referent,* and *expert.*
2. The instructor will present examples of publicly visible people such as those listed below and in a full-class discussion you will be asked to discuss what types of power each wields.

D. Instructions for Students
Identify which type(s) of power characterizes each of the following people:
1. The President of the United States
2. Any particular one of your instructors
3. The mayor of your hometown
4. Your college or university President or Chancellor
5. The director of your social work program
6. The administrative assistant in your social work program
7. Your state governor
8. A friendly well-liked supervisor of part-time supervisees working for minimum wage at Hal's Hot Dog Heaven (a short-order restaurant)

---

[7] See *EPAS* EP 2.1.7.

9.   A mean, disliked supervisor of part-time supervisees working for minimum wage at Hal's Hot Dog Heaven (the same short-order restaurant)

10.   The author of your favorite novel

Competencies/Practice Behaviors Exercise 7.6
It's Not Fair; It's Just Not Fair—The Problematic, Challenging Supervisor

---

Focus Competencies or Practice Behaviors:
- EP 2.1.1f   Use supervision and consultation
- EP 2.1.2c   Tolerate ambiguity in resolving ethical conflicts
- EP 2.1.3   Apply critical thinking to inform and communicate professional judgments
- EP 2.1.7b   Critique and apply knowledge to understand person and environment
- EP 2.1.10a   Substantively and affectively prepare for action with individuals, families, groups, organizations, and communities

A.   **Brief Description**
      You will be presented with a range of problematic supervisory situations and asked to discuss how they would handle these scenarios.

B.   **Objectives**
      You will:
      1.   Examine the use of supervision.
      2.   Discuss approaches for dealing with designated problems with supervisors.
      3.   Experience how ambiguity (in terms of having no perfect solutions) can be experienced in conflicts with supervisors.

C.   **Procedure**
      1.   Review the material on supervision, using supervision appropriately, and problems in supervision.
      2.   The following scenarios will be presented to the class and you will be asked to discuss how you might handle the situation.
      3.   Potential consequences of various alternatives will be discussed.

D.   **Instructions for Students**
      Read the following scenarios about adventures in supervision that depict problematic situations with supervisors. Discuss how the supervisee might handle each situation. What might be the consequences of the various alternatives?

Adventures in Supervision

What Would You Do?

The following scenarios are taken from actual supervisory experiences. Each involves real problems that could theoretically happen to you. In each case, think about how you would pursue some type of resolution with each supervisor.

Scenario A: Taking Your Credit

You are a school social worker in a large, urban high school. Your primary role is "to help students, families, teachers, and educational administrators deal with a range of problems that affect students" including "truancy, depression, withdrawal, aggressive or violent behavior, rebelliousness, and the effects of physical or emotional problems" (Gibelman, 1995, p. 175). In essence, you work with students to combat truancy, enhance academic performance, encourage responsible decision making, and prevent disasters such as student shootings. This allows numerous possibilities for development and implementation of creative projects.

You come up with what you consider a brilliant idea. What about starting a program where interested high school teens would provide tutoring, craft project supervision, and recreational activities for children living at a local homeless shelter?[a] This would not only furnish a needed community service, but also provide opportunities for youth to learn empathy, feel useful, and responsibly help others.

You briefly mention the idea to your supervisor, Harmony, for her approval. Without hesitation she gives you the go-ahead. You meet with personnel from the shelter, parents of some of the homeless children who may be involved, potential student participants, members of the Parent/Teacher Association at your school, and school administrators. You contact people from other communities that have similar programs and put in a significant amount of work writing up the proposal. Finally, you submit it to Harmony for her endorsement. She states, "I'll take it from here. Higher administration supports this."

You don't quite believe your ears. Does she really mean she's taking it over after all the work you put into it? That can't be. You reply, "Just say okay, and I'll start implementation. One of the first things will be to solicit student volunteers."

She responds, "No, you've got lots of other things to do. I'll take over now." You emphasize how the whole thing was your idea, how hard you've worked, and how you are *really* committed to carry out the plan. You hear yourself pleading with her. You suggest working on the project together.

"No," she confirms, "I'll do it. Don't worry about it anymore." You are devastated. Worse yet three days later, you see a big write-up about the project in the local newspaper giving Harmony all the credit. Your name isn't even mentioned.

What would you do?

Scenario B: The Communication Gap

You are a newly hired social worker for a unit of boys, ages 11 to 13, at a residential treatment center for youth with serious behavioral and emotional problems. Your responsibilities include counseling, group work, case management, some family counseling, and consultation with unit counseling staff concerning your unit's behavioral programming. Two of the dozen boys in the unit have been causing you particular trouble. They are late for your weekly counseling sessions, sometimes skipping them altogether. When you talk to them, they don't respond to your questions. Rather, they walk around the room, talk about how you don't know what you're doing, use pencils to pick holes in the furniture, and call you vulgar names.

You are at a loss regarding what to do with these two clients. You go into your weekly one-hour supervisory sessions and explain the situation to your supervisor. He makes a number of vague suggestions, such as recording some of your sessions, making home visits, and talking about the boys' behavior with them. By the end of your supervisory session, you feel you've gotten nowhere. You couldn't pin down any specific suggestions and still do not understand what you should do. You have difficulty understanding what your supervisor is saying. You can't "read" him. Sometimes when he makes a statement you don't know whether he expects you to laugh in response or to take him seriously and say, "Oh, gee, that's too bad."

What would you do?

Scenario C: The Angry Response

You are a social worker at a health care center (nursing home) with various clients who have been diagnosed as having a mental illness. Every six months, a treatment conference is held at which social workers, nurses, therapists (speech, occupational, physical), physicians, psychologists, and psychiatrists summarize clients' progress and make recommendations. It is your job to run the meeting and write the summary.

You are new at your job and are not familiar with how things are run at this agency. You find that during the meeting, the psychiatrist is very verbal. You would even describe him as "pushy." You feel intimidated and uncomfortable asserting your own opinions, which are somewhat opposed to his. His advanced education, status, and self-confident demeanor make you feel that his points are probably more important and valid than yours.

After the meeting, your supervisor, who was also in attendance, takes you aside. His face is red and his voice has a deadly, steel-like calm in it. He berates you for letting the psychiatrist take over the meeting. He surprises and upsets you so that you do not hear many of the specific things he says. You just know that he is furious with you and that he has implied or stated that you are incompetent. He walks off in a huff.

What would you do?

Scenario D: Gender Discrimination

You have the strong feeling that your supervisor, who is heterosexual and of the same gender as you, gives opposite-gender supervisees preferential treatment. For instance, the supervisor acts friendlier and more casual with them, directs more comments and questions to them during meetings, and seems to give them preference for their vacation choices. You have also heard they're getting higher raises when you feel your own work performance is at least as good as theirs, if not better.

What would you do?

Scenario E: Problems with Delegation

You are a caseworker for a social services agency in a rural county. Your job includes a wide range of social work practice, from investigating child abuse charges to working with families of truants to providing supplementary services to older adults so that they can remain in their own homes. You have a heavy caseload but feel very useful. In general, you really like your job.

The problem is that your supervisor insists on reading every letter and report you write before it goes out. You think this is a terribly time-consuming waste of effort. In many instances, it also delays your provision of service. Finally, you feel it's condescending and implies a lack of confidence in your professional abilities.

What would you do?

Scenario F: No Action

You are a social worker in a large urban community center serving multiple community needs. Services include counseling for emotional and behavior problems, provision of contraception, recreational activities for adults and youth, day care for children of working parents, meals for senior citizens, some health care, and various other services. Your job focuses primarily on counseling the center's clients, who are referred to you for this purpose. You enjoy your job and are proud of being a professional social worker.

The problem is another social worker who has his office next door. He has a similar job, but is assigned a different caseload and a slightly different range of responsibilities. The bottom line is that you seriously question his professional competence. You've observed him doing what you'd describe as "comic book therapy" with the children and adolescents on his caseload. In other words, his clients come in and select comic books from his vast collection instead of receiving any real form of counseling. He has boasted on several occasions that he went into social work only because somehow he was offered a scholarship.

One day you walk up to greet one of your clients, whom you unexpectedly see reading something in the center's waiting room. Your client, a fairly bright articulate boy of 13, places his hand over a portion of a picture in the book. You think to yourself how odd that is, because his hand is placed over the rear of a horse. He does look surprised to see you. He remarks that the horse's long white mane is pretty. You observe that the mane reaches the ground and extends along another foot. This also strikes you as peculiar. Finally, you ask him what the book is about. He sheepishly shows it to you. The picture depicts a castrated horse (hence, the elongated mane and tail due to hormonal changes). The book is titled *Washington Death Trips.* Among other items included in the book are pictures of dead babies in caskets, people who have butchered over five hundred chickens by hand for no reason, and various infamous murderers. You learn that your colleague loaned your client this book.

You are furious. Not only does this colleague offend your professionalism and your professional ethics, he has also had the gall to interfere with your client. You immediately go to your supervisor, who is also his supervisor, and complain about the incident. Your supervisor, a well-liked, easygoing, but knowledgeable and helpful person, hems and haws. You believe that your supervisor is afraid to confront your colleague.

What would you do?

Note

a. The idea for the program described in this vignette was adapted from one proposed by J. P. Kretzmann and J. L. McKnight in *Building Communities from the Inside Out* (Chicago: ACTA Publications, 1993, p. 41).

REFERENCES

Council on Social Work Education (CSWE). (2008). *Educational policy and accreditation standards (EPAS).* Alexandria, VA: Author. (Available at www.cswe.org.)

Daft, R. L., & Marcic, D. (2013). *Understanding management* (8th ed.). Mason, OH: South-Western.

Gibelman, M. (1995). *What social workers do.* Washington, DC: NASW Press.

Griffin, R. W., & Moorhead, G. (2012). *Organizational behavior: Managing people and organizations* (10th ed.). Mason, OH: South-Western.

Kretzmann, J. P., & McKnight, J. L. (1993). *Building communities from the inside out.* Chicago: ACTA Publications.

Chapter 7 Competencies/Practice Behaviors Exercises Assessment:

Name: _____ **Date:** _____

Supervisor's Name: _____

Focus Competencies/Practice Behaviors:
- EP 2.1.1   Identify as a professional social worker and conduct oneself accordingly
- EP 2.1.1f   Use supervision and consultation
- EP 2.1.2c   Tolerate ambiguity in resolving ethical conflicts
- EP 2.1.3   Apply critical thinking to inform and communicate professional judgments
- EP 2.1.4a   Recognize the extent to which a culture's structures and values may oppress, marginalize, alienate, or create or enhance privilege and power
- EP 2.1.5a   Understand forms and mechanisms of oppression and discrimination
- EP 2.1.7   Apply knowledge of human behavior and the social environment
- EP 2.1.7b   Critique and apply knowledge to understand person and environment
- EP 2.1.10   Engage, assess, intervene, and evaluate with individuals, families, groups, organizations, and communities
- EP 2.1.10a   Substantively and affectively prepare for action with individuals, families, groups, organizations, and communities

Instructions:

A.   Evaluate your work or your partner's work in the Focus Competencies/Practice Behaviors by completing the Competencies/Practice Behaviors Assessment form below

B.   What other Competencies/Practice Behaviors did you use to complete these Exercises? Be sure to record them in your assessments

1.	I have attained this competency/practice behavior (in the range of 81 to 100%)
2.	I have largely attained this competency/practice behavior (in the range of 61 to 80%)
3.	I have partially attained this competency/practice behavior (in the range of 41 to 60%)
4.	I have made a little progress in attaining this competency/practice behavior (in the range of 21 to 40%)
5.	I have made almost no progress in attaining this competency/practice behavior (in the range of 0 to 20%)

EPAS 2008 Core Competencies & Core Practice Behaviors	Student Self Assessment						Evaluator Feedback
Student and Evaluator Assessment Scale and Comments	0	1	2	3	4	5	Agree/Disagree/ Comments
EP 2.1.1 Identify as a Professional Social Worker and Conduct Oneself Accordingly:							
a. Advocate for client access to the services of social work							
b. Practice personal reflection and self-correction to assure continual professional development							
c. Attend to professional roles and boundaries							
d. Demonstrate professional demeanor in behavior, appearance, and communication							
e. Engage in career-long learning							
f. Use supervision and consultation							
EP 2.1.2 Apply Social Work Ethical Principles to Guide Professional Practice:							
a. Recognize and manage personal values in a way that allows professional values to guide practice							
b. Make ethical decisions by applying NASW Code of Ethics and, as applicable, of the IFSW/IASSW Ethics in Social Work, Statement of Principles							
c. Tolerate ambiguity in resolving ethical conflicts							
d. Apply strategies of ethical reasoning to arrive at principled decisions							
EP 2.1.3 Apply Critical Thinking to Inform and Communicate Professional Judgments:							
a. Distinguish, appraise, and integrate multiple sources of knowledge, including research-based knowledge and practice wisdom							
b. Analyze models of assessment, prevention, intervention, and evaluation							
c. Demonstrate effective oral and written communication in working with individuals, families, groups, organizations, communities, and colleagues							
EP 2.1.4 Engage Diversity and Difference in Practice:							
a. Recognize the extent to which a culture's structures and values may oppress, marginalize, alienate, or create or enhance privilege and power							
b. Gain sufficient self-awareness to eliminate the influence of personal biases and values in working with diverse groups							
c. Recognize and communicate their understanding of the importance of difference in shaping life experiences							
d. View themselves as learners and engage those with whom they work as informants							
EP 2.1.5 Advance Human Rights and Social and Economic Justice:							
a. Understand forms and mechanisms of oppression and discrimination							
b. Advocate for human rights and social and economic justice							
c. Engage in practices that advance social and economic justice							

EP 2.1.6 Engage in Research-Informed Practice and Practice-Informed Research:								
a.	Use practice experience to inform scientific inquiry							
b.	Use research evidence to inform practice							
EP 2.1.7 Apply Knowledge of Human Behavior and the Social Environment:								
a.	Utilize conceptual frameworks to guide the processes of assessment, intervention, and evaluation							
b.	Critique and apply knowledge to understand person and environment							
EP 2.1.8 Engage in Policy Practice to Advance Social and Economic Well-Being and to Deliver Effective Social Work Services:								
a.	Analyze, formulate, and advocate for policies that advance social well-being							
b.	Collaborate with colleagues and clients for effective policy action							
EP 2.1.9 Respond to Contexts that Shape Practice:								
a.	Continuously discover, appraise, and attend to changing locales, populations, scientific and technological developments, and emerging societal trends to provide relevant services							
b.	Provide leadership in promoting sustainable changes in service delivery and practice to improve the quality of social services							
EP 2.1.10 Engage, Assess, Intervene, and Evaluate with Individuals, Families, Groups, Organizations and Communities:								
a.	Substantively and affectively prepare for action with individuals, families, groups, organizations, and communities							
b.	Use empathy and other interpersonal skills							
c.	Develop a mutually agreed-on focus of work and desired outcomes							
d.	Collect, organize, and interpret client data							
e.	Assess client strengths and limitations							
f.	Develop mutually agreed-on intervention goals and objectives							
g.	Select appropriate intervention strategies							
h.	Initiate actions to achieve organizational goals							
i.	Implement prevention interventions that enhance client capacities							
j.	Help clients resolve problems							
k.	Negotiate, mediate, and advocate for clients							
l.	Facilitate transitions and endings							
m.	Critically analyze, monitor, and evaluate interventions							

Competencies/Practice Behaviors Exercise 8.1
Which Behavior Pattern is This?

Focus Competencies or Practice Behaviors:
- EP 2.1.4a Recognize the extent to which a culture's structures and values may oppress, marginalize, alienate, or create or enhance privilege and power
- EP 2.1.7b Critique and apply knowledge to understand person and environment

A. Brief Description

A series of vignettes are presented, reflecting various behavior patterns found in bureaucratic systems. You are then asked to identify and discuss which behavior pattern is dramatized in each vignette.

B. Objectives

You will:
1. "Critique and apply knowledge to understand person and environment" by appraising a range of vignettes concerning behavior patterns sometimes evident in bureaucratic systems.[1]
2. Examine the motivations behind each behavior pattern.

C. Procedure
1. Review the material on the six behavior patterns sometimes found in bureaucratic systems.
2. The instructor will read the vignettes presented below under "D. Instructions for Students" and initiate a discussion focusing on the following questions and issues concerning each vignette:
   a. Which behavior pattern is characterized by the vignette?
   b. What components of the vignette characterize that behavior pattern?
   c. What might be the motivations for people adopting such a behavior pattern?
   d. In what ways does the behavior pattern harm the agency and its ability to function effectively?

---

[1] See Council on Social Work Education (CSWE) *Educational Policy and Accreditation Standards (EPAS)* Educational Policy (EP) 2.1.7, ("Apply knowledge of human behavior and the social environment").

D. Instructions for Students

For each of the vignettes below, identify which of the six behavior patterns often encountered in bureaucratic systems apply (Knopf, 1979, pp. 33-36). The behavior patterns are:

1.	Warrior
2.	Gossip
3.	Complainer
4.	Dancer
5.	Machine
6.	Executioner

Vignette A: Barry hates rules. He likes to put his feet up on his desk and read the newspaper for a half hour when he gets to work (of course, only when his supervisor isn't around). He also likes to stay out of the other staff's petty conflicts. He just wants to get by as easily as possible and pick up the old paycheck every two weeks. Barry is a(n) _____.

Vignette B: Mary loves rules. She is a supervisor who thinks rules and the adherence to them make the world go round. Rules provide answers to confusing and stressful problems. Mary insists that her supervisees obey the rules to the letter. She doesn't want them to make mistakes by doing much thinking on their own. Mary is a(n) _____.

Vignette C: Larry is an agency supervisor. He thinks he is very important, in fact, much too important to be involved with this "inferior" agency. He's a "go-getter kind o' guy" who wants to get ahead in the worst way. He's good at "playing the game" so that agency administration doesn't realize how hostile toward it he really is. Precious, the agency assistant director who supervises Larry, had the nerve to suggest some improvements in his performance. Larry thinks Precious will be sorry for that. He knows how to rub her name in the dirt. Larry is a(n) _____.

Vignette D: Carrie loves to fight. She fights about agency policies. She fights about supervisory procedures. She fights about paperwork requirements. Her basic desire is to demolish "the system." Carrie is a(n) _____.

Vignette E: Gary loves to spread the word about everything that's wrong in the agency. He complains to colleagues, personal friends, and personnel from other agencies. Sometimes, he calls the newspaper and "narcs" on all the "unethical" and "illegal" things he feels the agency administration is doing. He especially despises the agency director, whom he feels treats him very unfairly. He has not received a merit raise for the past two years. Gary is a(n) _____.

Vignette F: Harry complains about everything inside the agency. The coffee's too strong or too weak. The office is too cold or too hot. His supervisor is too bossy, weak, or incompetent. The agency administration doesn't care about its staff. Everything is wrong. Harry only complains to his immediate colleagues inside the agency because he doesn't want to suffer any negative consequences from the administration. Harry is a(n) _____.

Competencies/Practice Behaviors Exercise 8.2
Management and Empowerment

Focus Competencies or Practice Behaviors:
- EP 2.1.1a Advocate for client access to the services of social work
- EP 2.1.2 Apply social work ethical principles to guide professional practice
- EP 2.1.7b Critique and apply knowledge to understand person and environment
- EP 2.1.8a Analyze, formulate, and advocate for policies that advance social well-being
- EP 2.1.10k Negotiate, mediate, and advocate for clients

A. **Brief Description**
You are presented with a case example of a distressed client and are asked to suggest how the organization might empower that client.

B. **Objectives**
You will:
1. "Critique and apply knowledge to understand person and environment" by examining how a client might be or not be empowered by an organization.[2]
2. Explore "ways social systems promote or deter people in maintaining or achieving health and well-being."[3]
3. "Attend to professional roles and boundaries."[4]
4. "Apply strategies of ethical reasoning to arrive at principled decisions."[5]
5. Propose means of client and employee empowerment.

C. **Procedure**
1. Review the material on client system empowerment by management.
2. The instructor will present students with the case example portrayed below.
3. In a full-class discussion, students will answer the questions posed below.

---

[2] See *EPAS* EP 2.1.7.
[3] See *EPAS* EP 2.1.7.
[4] See *EPAS* EP 2.1.1 ("Identify as a professional social worker and conduct oneself accordingly").
[5] See *EPAS* EP 2.1.2 ("Apply social work ethical principles to guide professional practice").

D.   Instructions for Students

1.   Your instructor will introduce the following case scenario of a distressed client. You then will participate in a discussion addressing the subsequent questions.

CASE SCENARIO:

Yoko is furious. She is the single mother of three young children and a client at Penniless County Department of Social Services. She is currently receiving public assistance and is enrolled in a work preparation program teaching her skills in food preparation.

She has tried to see her assigned social worker Gunter eight times without success. The man is simply never there. Twice she's tried to complain to a supervisor, but was cut off at the pass by secretarial sentries who adamantly declared that all supervisors were busy at the moment. They added she could make an appointment in three weeks or so.

Yoko's problem is that she discovered she hates food preparation and the training program in which she was arbitrarily placed. She wants to work and needs training, but couldn't it involve office or sales or anything but food preparation? She has little time to make a change. She will only qualify for a few more months of assistance before she is required to work and her assistance is terminated.

Yoko doesn't know who she can turn to. The agency has no client advisory group or formal appeal process for clients to use. Clients must work through their designated worker. Yoko feels frustrated, angry, and powerless.

---

2.   Address the following questions:

a.   How might the Department of Social Services' management improve "the system" to include procedures and opportunities for Yoko's empowerment?

b.   How might she be allowed better opportunities to voice her opinions, make her own decisions, and have direct access to people in power making decisions about her?

> **Competencies/Practice Behaviors Exercise 8.3**
> **Identifying Concepts in Total Quality Management**

Focus Competencies or Practice Behaviors:

- EP 2.1.7a   Utilize conceptual frameworks to guide the processes of assessment, intervention, and evaluation
- EP 2.1.7b   Critique and apply knowledge to understand person and environment

A.   Brief Description

You will match definitions with components of quality management. Ensuing discussion concerns the importance of quality treatment.

B. **Objectives**
   You will:
   1. "Critique and apply knowledge [about quality management] to understand person and environment."[6]
   2. "Utilize [the quality management] conceptual framework...to guide the processes" of assessing service provision in organizations.[7]

C. **Procedure**
   1. You will be provided with copies of or visual access to the matching exercise under "D. Instructions for Students."
   2. You will be allowed a few minutes to complete the exercise, after which the instructor will initiate a discussion with the class regarding the importance of each of these quality components.
   3. You will be asked to comment on your experiences as a customer, not necessarily with social services, but with commercial businesses. Have you had exceptionally bad experiences? Exceptionally good? What were your reactions?

D. **Instructions for Students**
   Match the following terms, all components of "quality" in management with their respective definitions:

   a. Accuracy
   b. Consistency
   c. Responsiveness
   d. Availability
   e. Perceived value
   f. Service experience

   1. _____ : The ease with which customers can obtain services.

   2. _____ : Service accuracy over time.

   3. _____ : The extent to which actual service provision matches customers' expectations.

   4. _____ : The extent to which the customers feel the service is worth it.

   5. _____ : The sum of the total treatment experience with all of its nuances and innuendoes.

   6. _____ : The timeliness of service provision.

---

[6] See *EPAS* EP 2.1.7.
[7] *See EPAS* EP 2.1.7.

Competencies/Practice Behaviors Exercise 8.4
Service Sins

Focus Competencies or Practice Behaviors:
- EP 2.1.1d   Demonstrate professional demeanor in behavior, appearance, and communication
- EP 2.1.3c   Demonstrate effective oral and written communication in working with individuals, families, groups, organizations, communities, and colleagues
- EP 2.1.7b   Critique and apply knowledge to understand person and environment
- EP 2.1.10a   Substantively and affectively prepare for action with individuals, families, groups, organizations, and communities
- EP 2.1.10b   Use empathy and other interpersonal skills

A.   Brief Description

In a full-class discussion, you will respond to a series of vignettes by identifying the sin of service portrayed and explain why.

B.   Objectives

You will "critique and apply knowledge to understand person and environment" by identifying the seven sins of service portrayed in one definition of quality management.[8]

C.   Procedure

1.   You will be presented with a series of scenarios. You will then identify which sin of service the scenario reflects and explain why.
2.   The seven sins of service will be defined.
3.   The instructor will read each of the "Shirley" scenarios portrayed under "D. Instructions for Students" below. You will be asked to identify the sin involved and explain why. (Note that one sin of service is intended to take precedence, although to various degrees more than one may be portrayed during the same interaction.)

D.   Instructions for Students

Read the introduction for Shirley and the seven scenarios portrayed below. Identify which sin of service is reflected and explain why.

---

[8] See *EPAS* EP 2.1.7.

a.   Apathy: Showing boredom with customer interactions and lack of concern.

b.   Brush-off: Getting rid of the customer if possible by ignoring her or forgetting to get back to her.

c.   Coldness: Expressing chilly hostility, curtness, unfriendliness, inconsiderateness, or impatience to customers.

d.   Condescension: Treating customers with a disdainful, patronizing attitude that implies you as the worker are more knowledgeable and, in essence, better than the customers.

e.   Robotism: Treating each customer identically without responding to individual differences.

f.   Rule book: Using the rule book to give the organization's rules and regulations absolute preference.

g.   Runaround: Stalling customers or sending them on "wild goose chases," thus wasting their time.

INTRODUCTION: Shirley works for a county agency in its financial assistance unit. Her job is to solicit financial information from people seeking financial assistance and other social services to determine their eligibility. It's 4:15 p.m. on a Friday; she only has 45 more minutes to go before she can finally get out of there and go home. She is exhausted and looking forward to a very big weekend. There are four people waiting in the small waiting room outside her office cubicle. Each has taken a number and is waiting for his or her turn.

Scenario #1:   Shirley takes forms on clipboards out to the waiting clients and instructs them all to complete the forms and turn them back in to her. She does not attend to the fact that one client holds a cane with a red tip and a seeing-eye dog sitting on the floor besides him.
Which sin(s) of service does this portray? Explain why.

Scenario #2:   Shirley is interviewing a client who states, "I'm having trouble understanding exactly what the questions on this form mean." Shirley replies, " Oh? It's really easy. All you have to do is use your head."
Which sin(s) of service does this portray? Explain why.

Scenario #3:   Shirley is interviewing her next client. As the client painfully explains his current financial plight, Shirley notices her thoughts have been drifting away, focusing on her upcoming big weekend. She first catches herself yawning and then says, "What was that you said again?"
Which sin(s) of service does this portray? Explain why.

Scenario #4: A client enters Shirley's third floor cubicle and asks where the agency's foster care unit is. Shirley responds, "Go back to the information desk at the entrance on the first floor. They'll tell you." The foster care unit, Shirley knows, is on her own floor. However, an explanation of how to reach it would take a minute or two.
Which sin(s) of service does this portray? Explain why.

Scenario #5: A client explains to Shirley how the client is experiencing especially difficult financial circumstances at this time and explains why. Shirley responds, "Unfortunately, those circumstances don't matter. Our policy is clear regarding the resources that are available to clients."
Which sin(s) of service does this portray? Explain why.

Scenario #6: Shirley leaves her office to get a cup of coffee and walks through the waiting area. A client stands up and says, "Excuse me, can I talk to you?" With a stone-faced expression, Shirley curtly replies, "Don't rush me. I'll be back in a few minutes."
Which sin(s) of service does this represent? Explain why.

Scenario #7: Shirley leaves her office to get a cup of coffee and walks through the waiting area. A client stands up and says, "Excuse me, can I talk to you?" Shirley smiles warmly and replies, "I'm sorry. I'll be back in a few minutes. Let's talk then." Shirley returns 45 minutes later at closing time.
Which sin(s) of service does this represent? Explain why.

Competencies/Practice Behaviors Exercise 8.5
Organizational Culture Investigation

Focus Competencies or Practice Behaviors:
- EP 2.1.3a   Distinguish, appraise, and integrate multiple sources of knowledge, including research-based knowledge and practice wisdom
- EP 2.1.7b   Critique and apply knowledge to understand person and environment
- EP 2.1.10a   Substantively and affectively prepare for action with individuals, families, groups, organizations, and communities

A.   **Brief Description**
You are provided a paper assignment involving a questionnaire format and asked to interview a social services employee to evaluate organizational culture. You are then asked to score the questionnaire results and summarize your impressions regarding the management approach adopted by the agency.

B.   Objectives

You will:
1.   "Critique and apply knowledge to understand person and environment" by soliciting information about a social services organization from an employee.[9]
2.   Assess the strengths and weaknesses of the management style manifested by that organization.

C.   Procedure
1.   You will be provided with copies of the questionnaire and 5-phase instructions listed below.
2.   Read the instructions.
3.   Ask any questions you might have about the assignment.

D.   Instructions for Students

Phase 1:   The two questionnaires below illustrate examples of the types of questions you can ask to evaluate organizational culture.   They compare two diverse types of organizational culture, traditional bureaucracy and a client/employee centered approach such as total quality management (TQM). This exercise's intent is to sensitize you to differences in organizational culture and to how it may significantly affect how you can function within an agency.

To complete the exercise, select a social services agency within your area. It may be large or small, public or private.   Any organizational structure may be assessed according to the variables identified below.

You may interview a direct services worker, a supervisor, or an administrator.   The intent of this questionnaire is not to arrive at a specific score to precisely define organizational culture.   Rather, it is to provide you with some thought-provoking information about what agency life can be like.

Phase 2:   Explain to the interviewee that your purpose is to investigate organizational culture and that honest answers to questions would be appreciated. Define organizational culture as it is presented in the text.   Give brief examples also presented in the text of traditional bureaucracy and TQM.   Instruct the interviewee to answer both questionnaires to the best of her ability, providing a score from one to five according to the following scale: (1) never; (2) infrequently; (3) sometimes; (4) frequently; and (5) always.   Record her/his responses below.

---

[9] See *EPAS* EP 2.1.7.

BUREAUCRATIC ORIENTATION QUESTIONNAIRE[10]

1. Most professional employees in this organization hold a clearly defined job with clearly designated responsibilities.

Never	Infrequently	Sometimes	Frequently	Always
1	2	3	4	5

2. Most professional employees in this organization and are told straightforwardly and specifically how that job should be accomplished.

Never	Infrequently	Sometimes	Frequently	Always
1	2	3	4	5

3. Supervisors closely scrutinize employees' work.

Never	Infrequently	Sometimes	Frequently	Always
1	2	3	4	5

4. The administration considers efficiency to be of the utmost importance.

Never	Infrequently	Sometimes	Frequently	Always
1	2	3	4	5

5. Decisions about agency policy and practice tend to be made by higher administration and flow from the top down.

Never	Infrequently	Sometimes	Frequently	Always
1	2	3	4	5

6. Power within the agency is held primarily by top executives.

Never	Infrequently	Sometimes	Frequently	Always
1	2	3	4	5

---

[10]Many of the questions listed below are derived from the conflicts posed by Knopf (1979) that occur between the orientations of helping professionals and bureaucratic systems.

7. Communication within the organization flows from the top down.

Never	Infrequently	Sometimes	Frequently	Always
1	2	3	4	5

8. There is little communication among horizontal units, that is, units of approximately equal status that perform different functions.

Never	Infrequently	Sometimes	Frequently	Always
1	2	3	4	5

9. The organization emphasizes a rigid structure of power and authority that works to maintain stability and the status quo.

Never	Infrequently	Sometimes	Frequently	Always
1	2	3	4	5

10. The organization and its administration consider adherence to specified rules and policies as very important.

Never	Infrequently	Sometimes	Frequently	Always
1	2	3	4	5

CUSTOMER/EMPLOYEE ORIENTATION QUESTIONNAIRE

1. The organization places primary importance on the client (customer) and on effective service to clients.

Never	Infrequently	Sometimes	Frequently	Always
1	2	3	4	5

2. The organization holds practitioners in high regard who provide services directly to clients.

Never	Infrequently	Sometimes	Frequently	Always
1	2	3	4	5

3. The organization's administrative structure is viewed primarily as a support system for clients and the direct service workers serving them.

Never	Infrequently	Sometimes	Frequently	Always
1	2	3	4	5

4. The organization's administration considers as its major goal quality of service such as consistency of service provision, responsiveness to clients' needs, and service availability.

Never	Infrequently	Sometimes	Frequently	Always
1	2	3	4	5

5. Organizational leadership seeks to empower agency practitioners so that they might do their jobs as effectively as possible.

Never	Infrequently	Sometimes	Frequently	Always
1	2	3	4	5

6. Professional employees are encouraged to provide input into how the organization is run.

Never	Infrequently	Sometimes	Frequently	Always
1	2	3	4	5

7. The organization values client feedback and incorporates it into improving service provision.

Never	Infrequently	Sometimes	Frequently	Always
1	2	3	4	5

8. Professional employees are encouraged to work together to improve service provision.

Never	Infrequently	Sometimes	Frequently	Always
1	2	3	4	5

9. Communication flow is open and frequent among most agency units.

Never	Infrequently	Sometimes	Frequently	Always
1	2	3	4	5

10. Professional employees feel that their input to upper levels of administration is valued and put to use.

Never	Infrequently	Sometimes	Frequently	Always
1	2	3	4	5

Phase 3: You may then ask the interviewee the following questions about the organization's culture and effectiveness.
1. How would you describe the organization's culture?
2. To what extent do you feel the organization's culture enhances or detracts from practitioners' ability to do their work effectively?
3. What are the strengths of the organization's culture?
4. What are the weaknesses of the organization's culture?
5. Ideally, what changes, if any, would you make in the organizational culture?

Phase 4: After the interview, add up the scores separately for each questionnaire and divide each by ten. The two average scores will range from 1 which reflects the organization's low commitment to the respective management style to 5 which indicates a very high commitment. You may find an inverse relationship between scores on the Bureaucratic and Customer/Employee Orientation questionnaires, demonstrating the contrasting goals of the two theoretical orientations.

Phase 5: Write a paper summarizing your results. Include the following:
a. Both questionnaire scores and a commentary about why they are what they are.
b. A summary of the interviewee's responses to questions posed in Phase 4.
c. Your own impressions concerning how the agency is functioning and what are its strengths and weaknesses.

Focus Competencies or Practice Behaviors:
- EP 2.1.1f   Use supervision and consultation
- EP 2.1.3a   Distinguish, appraise, and integrate multiple sources of knowledge, including research-based knowledge and practice wisdom
- EP 2.1.7b   Critique and apply knowledge to understand person and environment
- EP 2.1.10a   Substantively and affectively prepare for action with individuals, families, groups, organizations, and communities

A.   **Brief Description**

You are assigned a paper where you are asked to use critical thinking in the assessment and comparison of Total Quality Management and service leadership.

B.   **Objectives**

You will:

1.   "Apply critical thinking" by synthesizing and analyzing major concepts in two management styles.[11]
2.   Evaluate the pros and cons of each approach in addition to its potential effectiveness.

C.   **Procedure**

You will be asked to write a paper answering the following questions:

1.   What are the pros and cons of Total Quality Management?
2.   To what extent would you feel comfortable either being an employee or a manager in an organization employing Total Quality Management principles?
3.   What are the pros and cons of servant leadership?
4.   To what extent would you feel comfortable either being an employee or a manager in an organization employing servant leadership principles?
5.   Under which management style would you prefer to be employed? Explain why.

---

[11] See *EPAS* EP 2.1.3 ("Apply critical thinking to inform and communicate professional judgments").

Focus Competencies or Practice Behaviors:
- EP 2.1.1b   Practice personal reflection and self-correction to assure continual professional development
- EP 2.1.1d   Demonstrate professional demeanor in behavior, appearance, and communication
- EP 2.1.3c   Demonstrate effective oral and written communication in working with individuals, families, groups, organizations, communities, and colleagues
- EP 2.1.10b Use empathy and other interpersonal skills

A.   **Brief Description**
You are presented with vignettes portraying uncomfortable situations and asked to suggest aggressive, nonassertive, and assertive responses.

B.   **Objectives**
You will:
1.   Propose appropriate assertive responses for scenarios occurring in macro settings.
2.   Evaluate the potential benefits and costs of such responses.

C.   **Procedure**
1.   Review the material on appropriate assertiveness in the macro environment. Brief definitions are provided in the box below.

Brief Definitions Regarding Assertiveness

Nonassertive communication: Meek verbal and nonverbal behavior coming from a speaker who devalues herself completely, feeling the other person and what that person thinks are much more important than her own thoughts.

Aggressive communication: Bold and dominating verbal and nonverbal behavior whereby a speaker presses her point of view as taking precedence above all other points of view, considering only her own views important, not the views of others.

Assertive communication: Verbal and nonverbal behavior that permits a speaker to get her points across clearly and straightforwardly, taking into consideration both her own value and the values of whomever is receiving her message.

---

2.   Using a full-class discussion format or a small group format followed by a full-class discussion, you will be asked to respond assertively to the vignettes below.

D. **Instructions for Students**

Read each of the following and respond to the subsequent questions.

Scenario A: You are a social worker for Heterogeneous County Department of Social Services. Paperwork recording your activities with clients is due promptly the Monday following the last day of each month. For whatever reason, you simply forget to get it in by 5:00 p.m. Monday the day it's due. Your supervisor Enrique calls you at noon the next day. He raises his voice and reprimands, "You know that reports are due promptly so that funding is not jeopardized. How many times do I have to tell you that?"

Nonassertive Response:

Aggressive Response:

Assertive Response:

Costs and benefits of each type of response:

Scenario B: You work with a colleague who consistently comes late to your social work unit's biweekly meetings. He typically saunters leisurely into the meeting room with a cup of decaf in hand, noisily situates himself in a chair at the rectangular meeting table, and casually interrupts whomever is speaking, asking for a brief review of what he missed. You are sick and tired of such rude, time-wasting behavior.

Nonassertive Response:

Aggressive Response:

Assertive Response:

Costs and benefits of each type of response:

Scenario C: You represent your social services agency at a community meeting where twelve community residents and five workers from other agencies are discussing what additional social services the community needs. Some possible grant funding has become available to develop services. The person chairing the meeting asks for input from each person present except you. Apparently, she simply overlooked that you had not gotten an opportunity to speak.

Nonassertive Response:

Aggressive Response:

Assertive Response:

Costs and benefits of each type of response:

Scenario D: Mohammed, a school social worker, applies for a state grant to start a summer activity program for adolescents in an urban neighborhood. Although he has already solicited support from his direct supervisor and from the school board, a principal from another school in the district objects to Mohammed's proposal: "Trying to get money for that project is inappropriate. It will result in significant differences in services between one school district and another, which is completely unfair. I think we should forget the idea."

Nonassertive Response:

Aggressive Response:

Assertive Response:

Costs and benefits of each type of response:

Scenario E: Audrey directs a group home for adults with physical disabilities. The home is run by a conservative religious organization which has publicly declared its anti-abortion stance. Her direct supervisor, the organization's director, is also strongly anti-abortion. Audrey, however, maintains a pro-choice position.

   A pro-choice rally is being held this weekend, and Audrey plans to attend and participate. She even expects to carry a pro-choice banner and march in a planned procession through the main area of town. Audrey's supervisor finds out about her plans, calls her aside, and says, "I forbid you to participate in that rally. Our agency has a reputation to maintain, and I won't allow you to jeopardize it."

Nonassertive Response:

Aggressive Response:

Assertive Response:

Costs and benefits of each type of response:

Scenario F: Hiroko is a public assistance worker for a large county bureaucracy. She is very dedicated to her job and often spends extra time with clients to make certain that they receive all possible benefits. Her colleague Bill, who has the same job title, tells Hiroko, "Either you're a fool and a drudge to work overtime like that, or you're trying to be a 'star' to feed your ego."

Nonassertive Response:

Aggressive Response:

Assertive Response:

Costs and benefits of each type of response:

Competencies/Practice Behaviors Exercise 8.8
Enhancing Assertiveness

Focus Competencies or Practice Behaviors:
- EP 2.1.1b   Practice personal reflection and self-correction to assure continual professional development
- EP 2.1.1d   Demonstrate professional demeanor in behavior, appearance, and communication
- EP 2.1.3c   Demonstrate effective oral and written communication in working with individuals, families, groups, organizations, communities, and colleagues
- EP 2.1.10b   Use empathy and other interpersonal skills

A.   **Brief Description**
You are asked to review situations in which they might behave more assertively.

B.   **Objectives**
You will:
1.   Identify situations where they did not act assertively and contrast these with situations where role models acted assertively.
2.   Propose assertive responses for relevant situations.

C.   **Procedure**
1. Review the material on assertiveness and assertiveness training.

2. Either in a full-class discussion in small groups followed by a full-class discussion, or as an individual assignment, discuss the following vignettes and propose two empathic responses for each.

D.   **Instructions for Students**

    1.   Recall a situation in which you could have acted more assertively. Perhaps you were too nonassertive or too aggressive. Describe the situation below.

    2.   Analyze the way you reacted in this situation. Critically examine both your verbal and nonverbal behavior. Describe and explain that behavior.

    3.   Choose a role model for assertive behavior in a situation similar to the one you have described. Identify the person you've chosen, then describe what happened and how she reacted assertively.

    4.   Identify two or three other assertive verbal and nonverbal responses that you could have employed in the situation you described.

    5.   Imagine yourself acting assertively in the situation you described. Explain what you would say and do.

    6.   After you have completed these five steps, try behaving assertively in real life. Continue practicing until assertiveness becomes part of your personal interactive style. Give yourself a pat on the back when you succeed in becoming more assertive. Be patient with yourself—it's not easy to change long-standing patterns of behavior

---

Competencies/Practice Behaviors Exercise 8.9
Resolving Conflicts

Focus Competencies or Practice Behaviors:

- EP 2.1.1b   Practice personal reflection and self-correction to assure continual professional development
- EP 2.1.1d   Demonstrate professional demeanor in behavior, appearance, and communication
- EP 2.1.3c   Demonstrate effective oral and written communication in working with individuals, families, groups, organizations, communities, and colleagues
- EP 2.1.10b Use empathy and other interpersonal skills

A.   **Brief Description**

You will identify a conflict situation in which they were involved and apply the steps of conflict resolution to it.

B.   **Objectives**

You will:

1. Explore the dimensions of conflict.
2. Apply the steps of conflict resolution to your own situations.

C. **Procedure**

1. Review the material on confrontation and conflict resolution. A *confrontation* is a face-to-face encounter where people come together with opposing opinions, perspectives, or ideas in order to scrutinize or compare them. See the material summarized in the box below on conflict resolution.

Steps in Conflict Resolution

The following seven steps of conflict resolution are proposed (Ivey & Ivey, 2008; Johnson, 2009):

Step 1: *Confront the opponent.* First, clearly identify and examine your personal goals. Second, keep in mind that it's important to nurture your relationship with your opponent.

Step 2: *Establish common ground.* Establish an acceptable definition of the problem that should make neither you nor your opponent defensive or resistant to compromise. Emphasize how important the issue is to both of you.

Step 3: Recognize the importance of maintaining communication with your opponent(s) in the conflict. Use the good communication techniques you have learned including the following (Sheafor and Horejsi, 2012, pp. 382-383):

    a. Do not begin a confrontation when you're angry.
    b. Do not enter into a conflict unless you have a clearly established reason for doing so.
    c. If you absolutely despise your opponent or have immense difficulty reaching for any positive, empathic feelings about him, do not confront him.
    d. Include positive statements and feedback along with the negative aspects of confrontation.
    e. Be certain to explain your concerns regarding the conflict in a descriptive, "nonjudgmental" manner (Sheafor & Horejsi, 2012, p. 267).
    f. Supply relevant data in support of your stance.
    g. An additional suggestion is to use "I-messages" frequently.

Step 4: *Emphasize your own willingness to work with your opponent to find a mutually satisfactory solution.* To minimize disagreement (or at least to develop a viable plan of action) stress whatever you and your opponent have in common.

Step 5: *Empathize with your opponent.* Think carefully about why she thinks, feels, or acts as she does.

Step 6: *Evaluate both your own and your opponent's motivation to address the conflict.* Is it worthwhile to expend the energy necessary to resolve this conflict?

> **Step 7:** Come to some mutual agreement by following these five suggestions (Johnson, 2009).
> a. Articulate exactly what your agreement entails.
> b. Indicate how you will behave toward the other person in the future as compared to in the past.
> c. Indicate how the other person has agreed to behave toward you.
> d. Agree on ways of addressing any future difficulties (such as might arise if you or the other person violates the agreement)
> e. Decide how and when you and the other person will meet to continue your cooperative behavior and to minimize future conflict.

2. Either in a full-class discussion or in small groups followed by a full-class discussion, answer the following questions in D. below.

D. Instructions for Students

Recall a conflict in which you have been involved. For the purposes of this exercise, it may be work-related, school-related, or personal. Answer the following questions:

1. Describe the conflict in detail. Who was involved? What was the issue? Explain the positions taken by the opposing sides. What were the circumstances of the actual confrontation?

2. Did you follow the suggestions in Step 1 for beginning a confrontation—that is, did you identify your goals and nurture your relationship with your opponent? What, if anything, could you have done differently to improve your handling of this conflict?

3. Did you follow Step 2 by finding some common ground with your opponent? What, if anything, could you have done differently to discover some common ground?

4. Did you follow Step 3 by maintaining communication with your opponent? What, if anything, could you have done differently to improve communication?

5. Did you follow Step 4 by indicating your willingness to cooperate with your opponent? What, if anything, could you have done differently to demonstrate this willingness?

6. Did you follow Step 5 by empathizing with your opponent and trying to understand his or her perspective? What, if anything, could you have done differently to achieve this empathy and understanding?

7. Did you follow Step 6 by evaluating both your own and your opponent's motivations in this conflict? What, if anything, could you have done differently to discern and evaluate those motives?

8. Did you follow Step 7 by arriving at some mutually satisfactory agreement? What, if anything, could you have done differently to make such an agreement possible?

REFERENCES

Council on Social Work Education (CSWE). (2008). *Educational policy and accreditation standards (EPAS)*. Alexandria, VA: Author. (Available at www.cswe.org.)

Ivey, A. E., & Ivey, M. B. (2008). *Essentials of intentional interviewing: Counseling in a multicultural world*. Belmont, CA: Brooks/Cole.

Johnson, D. W. (2009). *Reaching out: Interpersonal effectiveness and self-actualization* (10th ed.). Upper Saddle River, NJ: Pearson.

Knopf, R. (1979). *Surviving the BS (Bureaucratic System)*. Wilmington, NC: Mandala Press

Sheafor, B. W., & Horejsi, C. R. (2012). *Techniques and guidelines for social work practice* (9th ed.). Boston: Allyn & Bacon.

Chapter 8 Competencies/Practice Behaviors Exercises Assessment:

Name: _____ **Date:** _____

Supervisor's Name: _____

Focus Competencies/Practice Behaviors:

- EP 2.1.1a   Advocate for client access to the services of social work
- EP 2.1.1b   Practice personal reflection and self-correction to assure continual professional development
- EP 2.1.1d   Demonstrate professional demeanor in behavior, appearance, and communication
- EP 2.1.1f   Use supervision and consultation
- EP 2.1.2   Apply social work ethical principles to guide professional practice
- EP 2.1.3a   Distinguish, appraise, and integrate multiple sources of knowledge, including research-based knowledge and practice wisdom
- EP 2.1.3c   Demonstrate effective oral and written communication in working with individuals, families, groups, organizations, communities, and colleagues
- EP 2.1.4a   Recognize the extent to which a culture's structures and values may oppress, marginalize, alienate, or create or enhance privilege and power
- EP 2.1.7a   Utilize conceptual frameworks to guide the processes of assessment, intervention, and evaluation
- EP 2.1.7b   Critique and apply knowledge to understand person and environment
- EP 2.1.8a   Analyze, formulate, and advocate for policies that advance social well-being
- EP 2.1.10a   Substantively and affectively prepare for action with individuals, families, groups, organizations, and communities
- EP 2.1.10b   Use empathy and other interpersonal skills
- EP 2.1.10k   Negotiate, mediate, and advocate for clients

Instructions:

A.   Evaluate your work or your partner's work in the Focus Competencies/Practice Behaviors by completing the Competencies/Practice Behaviors Assessment form below

B.   What other Competencies/Practice Behaviors did you use to complete these Exercises? Be sure to record them in your assessments

1.	I have attained this competency/practice behavior (in the range of 81 to 100%)
2.	I have largely attained this competency/practice behavior (in the range of 61 to 80%)
3.	I have partially attained this competency/practice behavior (in the range of 41 to 60%)
4.	I have made a little progress in attaining this competency/practice behavior (in the range of 21 to 40%)
5.	I have made almost no progress in attaining this competency/practice behavior (in the range of 0 to 20%)

EPAS 2008 Core Competencies & Core Practice Behaviors	Student Self Assessment						Evaluator Feedback
Student and Evaluator Assessment Scale and Comments	0	1	2	3	4	5	Agree/Disagree /Comments
EP 2.1.1 Identify as a Professional Social Worker and Conduct Oneself Accordingly:							
a. Advocate for client access to the services of social work							
b. Practice personal reflection and self-correction to assure continual professional development							
c. Attend to professional roles and boundaries							
d. Demonstrate professional demeanor in behavior, appearance, and communication							
e. Engage in career-long learning							
f. Use supervision and consultation							
EP 2.1.2 Apply Social Work Ethical Principles to Guide Professional Practice:							
a. Recognize and manage personal values in a way that allows professional values to guide practice							
b. Make ethical decisions by applying NASW Code of Ethics and, as applicable, of the IFSW/IASSW Ethics in Social Work, Statement of Principles							
c. Tolerate ambiguity in resolving ethical conflicts							
d. Apply strategies of ethical reasoning to arrive at principled decisions							
EP 2.1.3 Apply Critical Thinking to Inform and Communicate Professional Judgments:							
a. Distinguish, appraise, and integrate multiple sources of knowledge, including research-based knowledge and practice wisdom							
b. Analyze models of assessment, prevention, intervention, and evaluation							
c. Demonstrate effective oral and written communication in working with individuals, families, groups, organizations, communities, and colleagues							
EP 2.1.4 Engage Diversity and Difference in Practice:							
a. Recognize the extent to which a culture's structures and values may oppress, marginalize, alienate, or create or enhance privilege and power							
b. Gain sufficient self-awareness to eliminate the influence of personal biases and values in working with diverse groups							
c. Recognize and communicate their understanding of the importance of difference in shaping life experiences							
d. View themselves as learners and engage those with whom they work as informants							
EP 2.1.5 Advance Human Rights and Social and Economic Justice:							
a. Understand forms and mechanisms of oppression and discrimination							
b. Advocate for human rights and social and economic justice							
c. Engage in practices that advance social and economic justice							

EP 2.1.6 Engage in Research-Informed Practice and Practice-Informed Research:							
a.	Use practice experience to inform scientific inquiry						
b.	Use research evidence to inform practice						
EP 2.1.7 Apply Knowledge of Human Behavior and the Social Environment:							
a.	Utilize conceptual frameworks to guide the processes of assessment, intervention, and evaluation						
b.	Critique and apply knowledge to understand person and environment						
EP 2.1.8 Engage in Policy Practice to Advance Social and Economic Well-Being and to Deliver Effective Social Work Services:							
a.	Analyze, formulate, and advocate for policies that advance social well-being						
b.	Collaborate with colleagues and clients for effective policy action						
EP 2.1.9 Respond to Contexts that Shape Practice:							
a.	Continuously discover, appraise, and attend to changing locales, populations, scientific and technological developments, and emerging societal trends to provide relevant services						
b.	Provide leadership in promoting sustainable changes in service delivery and practice to improve the quality of social services						
EP 2.1.10 Engage, Assess, Intervene, and Evaluate with Individuals, Families, Groups, Organizations and Communities:							
a.	Substantively and affectively prepare for action with individuals, families, groups, organizations, and communities						
b.	Use empathy and other interpersonal skills						
c.	Develop a mutually agreed-on focus of work and desired outcomes						
d.	Collect, organize, and interpret client data						
e.	Assess client strengths and limitations						
f.	Develop mutually agreed-on intervention goals and objectives						
g.	Select appropriate intervention strategies						
h.	Initiate actions to achieve organizational goals						
i.	Implement prevention interventions that enhance client capacities						
j.	Help clients resolve problems						
k.	Negotiate, mediate, and advocate for clients						
l.	Facilitate transitions and endings						
m.	Critically analyze, monitor, and evaluate interventions						

Chapter 9
Communities in the Social Environment: Theories and Concepts

Competencies/Practice Behaviors Exercise 9.1
Comparing and Contrasting Community Theories

Focus Competencies or Practice Behaviors:
- EP 2.1.3a   Distinguish, appraise, and integrate multiple sources of knowledge, including research-based knowledge and practice wisdom
- EP 2.1.4a   Recognize the extent to which a culture's structures and values may oppress, marginalize, alienate, or create or enhance privilege and power
- EP 2.1.7a   Utilize conceptual frameworks to guide the processes of assessment, intervention, and evaluation
- EP 2.1.7b   Critique and apply knowledge to understand person and environment

A.   **Brief Description**
Compare and contrast eight theoretical perspectives on communities.

B.   **Objectives**
You will:
1.   "Utilize conceptual frameworks [inherent in eight theoretical perspectives on communities] to guide the processes" of assessing communities.[1]
2.   "Critique and apply knowledge to understand person and environment" by examining the similarities and differences among the five approaches.[2]

C.   **Procedure**
1.   Review the material on theoretical perspectives on communities.
2.   The class will be divided into small groups of four to six.
3.   The groups will be asked to discuss the subsequent questions, select a group representative, and be prepared to report to the entire class the small group's findings.
4.   After about 20 minutes, the small groups will be asked to terminate their discussions and participate in a full-class discussion.
5.   A representative from each group will be asked to share her or his summary of the discussion. Comments will be encouraged from all class members.

---

[1] See Council on Social Work Education (CSWE) *Educational Policy and Accreditation Standards (EPAS)* Educational Policy (EP) 2.1.7, ("Apply knowledge of human behavior and the social environment").
[2] See *EPAS* EP 2.1.7.

D.   **Instructions for Students**
      1.   Identify the primary concepts involved in each of the following theoretical perspectives on communities:

      a.   Social systems
      b.   Human ecology
      c.   Social-psychological
      d.   Structural
      e.   Functionalist
      f.   Conflict
      g.   Symbolic interactionist
      h.   Empowerment

      2.   Describe the similarities and differences among the five perspectives.

Competencies/Practice Behaviors Exercise 9.2
Describing your Membership in Nongeographical Communities

Focus Competencies or Practice Behaviors:
- EP 2.1.1b   Practice personal reflection and self-correction to assure continual professional development
- EP 2.1.7b   Critique and apply knowledge to understand person and environment

A.   **Brief Description**
      Form small groups and discuss various aspects, similarities, and differences of the various non-geographical communities to which you belong.

B.   **Objectives**
      You will:
      1.   "Critique and apply knowledge to understand person and environment" by exploring the meaning of non-geographical community.[3]
      2.   Examine the non-geographical communities to which you belong.
      3.   Assess the strengths and weaknesses of membership in non-geographical communities.

C.   **Procedure**
      1.   Review the content on non-geographical communities.
      2.   Identify and write down the various nongeographical communities to which you belong (e.g., professional, spiritual, ethnic, racial, sexual orientation).
      3.   The instructor will initiate a full-class discussion regarding the nongeographical communities to which you belong.
      4.   Subsequently, you will address the questions posed below.

---

[3] See *EPAS* EP 2.1.7.

D.   **Instructions for Students**
  1.   Your instructor will ask you to identify and write down the non-geographical communities in which you belong. Class discussion will then focus on the various types.

  2.   Address the following questions:
    -    What are the strengths of the community to which you belong?
    -    What are the weaknesses inherent in that community?
    -    What are the reasons for belonging to that community?
    -    How does membership in that community affect your life?

Competencies/Practice Behaviors Exercise 9.3
Describing your Geographical Community

Focus Competencies or Practice Behaviors:
  - EP 2.1.1b   Practice personal reflection and self-correction to assure continual professional development
  - EP 2.1.7b   Critique and apply knowledge to understand person and environment

A.   **Brief Description**
  Form small groups and discuss various aspects including similarities and differences among your communities of origin.

B.   **Objectives**
  You will:
  1.   "Critique and apply knowledge to understand person and environment" by assessing your own communities of origin.[4]
  2.   Identify various dimensions of your geographical communities of origin.
  3.   Compare and contrast geographical communities.

C.   **Procedure**
  1.   Review the material on geographical communities.
  2.   The class will be divided into small groups of four to six.
  3.   The groups will be asked to discuss a number of questions concerning their home geographical communities. Each group should select a group representative who will take notes summarizing the similarities and differences among their communities and share these with the entire class.
  4.   Before beginning, the instructor will read the questions posed below.

---

[4] See *EPAS* EP 2.1.7.

5.   After about 20 minutes, the small groups will be asked to terminate their discussions and participate in a full-class discussion.

6.   A representative from each group will be asked to share her or his summary of community similarities and differences. Comments will be encouraged from other class members.

D.   Instructions for Students

1.   To the best of your ability, answer the following questions about the community you come from:

    a.   What is the population size?

    b.   What is the population density?

    c.   How heterogeneous is the community with respect to residents' socioeconomic status, racial/ethnic background, and age range?

    d.   Is your home community an urban community (metropolitan or micropolitan) or a smaller community (a small city, a small town, a bedroom community, an institutional community, a reservation community, or rural community)?

    e.   How would you describe this community in terms of its basic characteristics (for example, comfortable, crowded, sparsely populated, middle-class, poor)?

2.   Within your group, discuss the similarities and differences among your communities of origin.

Competencies/Practice Behaviors Exercise 9.4
The Ethics of Theory

Focus Competencies or Practice Behaviors:

- EP 2.1.2b   Make ethical decisions by applying standards of the National Association of Social Workers Code of Ethics and, as applicable, of the International Federation of Social Workers/International Association of Schools of Social Work Ethics in Social Work, Statement of Principles

- EP 2.1.7b   Critique and apply knowledge to understand person and environment

A.   Brief Description

A full-class discussion addresses the ethics of functionalist theory, homelessness, and social service organizations.

B.   Objectives

You will:

1. "Apply strategies of ethical reasoning to arrive at principled decisions" concerning the ethics of functionalist theory and how it relates to social work values.[5]
2. "Make ethical decisions by applying standards of the National Association of Social Workers Code of Ethics."[6]
3. Recognize the difficulty and complexity concerning the "ambiguity in resolving ethical conflicts."[7]

C. **Procedure**
1. Review the content on functionalist theory and the basic values inherent in the *NASW Code of Ethics* (the latter of which are portrayed in the box below).

The six core values in the *NASW Code of Ethics* include (NASW, 1999):
1. *Service:* Providing help, resources, and benefits so that people may achieve their maximum potential.
2. *Social justice:* Upholding the condition that in a perfect world, all citizens would have identical "rights, protection, opportunities, obligations, and social benefits" regardless of their backgrounds and membership in diverse groups (Barker, 2003, pp. 404-405).
3. *Dignity and worth of the person:* Holding in high esteem and appreciating individual value.
4. *Importance of human relationships:* Valuing the dynamic reciprocal interactions between social workers and clients, including how they communicate, think and feel about each other, and behave toward each other.
5. *Integrity:* Maintaining trustworthiness and sound adherence to moral ideals.
6. *Competence:* Having the necessary skills and abilities to perform work with clients effectively.

---

2. The instructor will lead a full-class discussion addressing the following questions:
   a. To what extent do you think it is ethical to view the social problem of homelessness from a functionalist perspective that focuses on its positives? Explain.
   b. To what extent are "social service agencies, religious organizations, and community groups and service workers" dependent on the homeless for their existence (Leon-Guerrero, 2011, p. 14)?

---

[5] See *EPAS* EP 2.1.2 ("Apply social work ethical principles to guide professional practice").
[6] See *EPAS* EP 2.1.2.
[7] See *EPAS* EP 2.1.2.

Focus Competencies or Practice Behaviors:

- EP 2.1.3a Distinguish, appraise, and integrate multiple sources of knowledge, including research-based knowledge and practice wisdom
- EP 2.1.7a Utilize conceptual frameworks to guide the processes of assessment, intervention, and evaluation
- EP 2.1.7b Critique and apply knowledge to understand person and environment

A. Brief Description

In small groups, compare and contrast a range of theories about communities.

B. Objectives

You will:

1. "Critique and apply knowledge to understand person and environment" by assessing similarities and differences among various community theories.[8]
2. Use critical thinking to "distinguish, appraise, and integrate multiple sources of knowledge" concerning conceptual frameworks about communities.[9]

C. Procedure

1. Review the material on systems, human ecology, social-psychological, structural, functionalist, and conflict theories with respect to communities.
2. The class will break into small groups of four to six. The groups will be instructed to prepare themselves to participate in a subsequent full-class discussion.
3. Choose two of these theories and address the following questions:
    a. What are the similarities and differences between two theories (that may include systems, human ecology, social-psychological, structural, functionalist, and conflict)?
    b. How might each theory apply to social service organizations and generalist social work practice?
4. You will be asked to return to a full-class discussion regarding your findings.

---

[8] See *EPAS* EP 2.1.7.

[9] See *EPAS* EP 2.1.3 ("Apply critical thinking to inform and communicate professional judgments").

REFERENCES

Barker, R. L. (2003). *The social work dictionary* (5th ed.). Washington, DC: NASW Press.

Council on Social Work Education (CSWE). (2008). *Educational policy and accreditation standards (EPAS).* Alexandria, VA: Author. (Available at www.cswe.org.)

Leon-Guerrero, A. (2011). *Social problems: Community, policy, and social action* (2nd ed.). Los Angeles: Pine Forge.

National Association of Social Workers (NASW). (1999). *Code of ethics.* Washington, DC: Author.

Chapter 9 Competencies/Practice Behaviors Exercises Assessment:

Name: _____ **Date:** _____

Supervisor's Name: _____

Focus Competencies/Practice Behaviors:
- EP 2.1.1b   Practice personal reflection and self-correction to assure continual professional development
- EP 2.1.2b   Make ethical decisions by applying standards of the National Association of Social Workers Code of Ethics and, as applicable, of the International Federation of Social Workers/International Association of Schools of Social Work Ethics in Social Work, Statement of Principles
- EP 2.1.3a   Distinguish, appraise, and integrate multiple sources of knowledge, including research-based knowledge and practice wisdom
- EP 2.1.4a   Recognize the extent to which a culture's structures and values may oppress, marginalize, alienate, or create or enhance privilege and power
- EP 2.1.7a   Utilize conceptual frameworks to guide the processes of assessment, intervention, and evaluation
- EP 2.1.7b   Critique and apply knowledge to understand person and environment

Instructions:
A.   Evaluate your work or your partner's work in the Focus Competencies/Practice Behaviors by completing the Competencies/Practice Behaviors Assessment form below
B.   What other Competencies/Practice Behaviors did you use to complete these Exercises? Be sure to record them in your assessments

1.	I have attained this competency/practice behavior (in the range of 81 to 100%)
2.	I have largely attained this competency/practice behavior (in the range of 61 to 80%)
3.	I have partially attained this competency/practice behavior (in the range of 41 to 60%)
4.	I have made a little progress in attaining this competency/practice behavior (in the range of 21 to 40%)
5.	I have made almost no progress in attaining this competency/practice behavior (in the range of 0 to 20%)

EPAS 2008 Core Competencies & Core Practice Behaviors							Student Self Assessment			Evaluator Feedback
Student and Evaluator Assessment Scale and Comments	0	1	2	3	4	5				Agree/Disagree /Comments
EP 2.1.1 Identify as a Professional Social Worker and Conduct Oneself Accordingly:										
a. Advocate for client access to the services of social work										
b. Practice personal reflection and self-correction to assure continual professional development										
c. Attend to professional roles and boundaries										

d.	Demonstrate professional demeanor in behavior, appearance, and communication						
e.	Engage in career-long learning						
f.	Use supervision and consultation						
EP 2.1.2 Apply Social Work Ethical Principles to Guide Professional Practice:							
a.	Recognize and manage personal values in a way that allows professional values to guide practice						
b.	Make ethical decisions by applying NASW Code of Ethics and, as applicable, of the IFSW/IASSW Ethics in Social Work, Statement of Principles						
c.	Tolerate ambiguity in resolving ethical conflicts						
d.	Apply strategies of ethical reasoning to arrive at principled decisions						
EP 2.1.3 Apply Critical Thinking to Inform and Communicate Professional Judgments:							
a.	Distinguish, appraise, and integrate multiple sources of knowledge, including research-based knowledge and practice wisdom						
b.	Analyze models of assessment, prevention, intervention, and evaluation						
c.	Demonstrate effective oral and written communication in working with individuals, families, groups, organizations, communities, and colleagues						
EP 2.1.4 Engage Diversity and Difference in Practice:							
a.	Recognize the extent to which a culture's structures and values may oppress, marginalize, alienate, or create or enhance privilege and power						
b.	Gain sufficient self-awareness to eliminate the influence of personal biases and values in working with diverse groups						
c.	Recognize and communicate their understanding of the importance of difference in shaping life experiences						
d.	View themselves as learners and engage those with whom they work as informants						
EP 2.1.5 Advance Human Rights and Social and Economic Justice:							
a.	Understand forms and mechanisms of oppression and discrimination						
b.	Advocate for human rights and social and economic justice						
c.	Engage in practices that advance social and economic justice						
EP 2.1.6 Engage in Research-Informed Practice and Practice-Informed Research:							
a.	Use practice experience to inform scientific inquiry						
b.	Use research evidence to inform practice						
EP 2.1.7 Apply Knowledge of Human Behavior and the Social Environment:							
a.	Utilize conceptual frameworks to guide the processes of assessment, intervention, and evaluation						
b.	Critique and apply knowledge to understand person and environment						

EP 2.1.8 Engage in Policy Practice to Advance Social and Economic Well-Being and to Deliver Effective Social Work Services:							
a.	Analyze, formulate, and advocate for policies that advance social well-being						
b.	Collaborate with colleagues and clients for effective policy action						
EP 2.1.9 Respond to Contexts that Shape Practice:							
a.	Continuously discover, appraise, and attend to changing locales, populations, scientific and technological developments, and emerging societal trends to provide relevant services						
b.	Provide leadership in promoting sustainable changes in service delivery and practice to improve the quality of social services						
EP 2.1.10 Engage, Assess, Intervene, and Evaluate with Individuals, Families, Groups, Organizations and Communities:							
a.	Substantively and affectively prepare for action with individuals, families, groups, organizations, and communities						
b.	Use empathy and other interpersonal skills						
c.	Develop a mutually agreed-on focus of work and desired outcomes						
d.	Collect, organize, and interpret client data						
e.	Assess client strengths and limitations						
f.	Develop mutually agreed-on intervention goals and objectives						
g.	Select appropriate intervention strategies						
h.	Initiate actions to achieve organizational goals						
i.	Implement prevention interventions that enhance client capacities						
j.	Help clients resolve problems						
k.	Negotiate, mediate, and advocate for clients						
l.	Facilitate transitions and endings						
m.	Critically analyze, monitor, and evaluate interventions						

Chapter 10
Assessment of Geographic Communities and Empowerment

Competencies/Practice Behaviors Exercise 10.1
Identifying Sources of Power

Focus Competencies or Practice Behaviors:
- EP 2.1.4a   Recognize the extent to which a culture's structures and values may oppress, marginalize, alienate, or create or enhance privilege and power
- EP 2.1.7b   Critique and apply knowledge to understand person and environment

A.   **Brief Description**
      You will appraise the potential sources of power for a range of individuals holding various positions and having different levels of status.

B.   **Objectives**
      You will:
      1.   "Critique and apply knowledge [about sources of personal power for various individuals] to understand person and environment."[1]

C.   **Procedure**
      1.   Review the material on sources of power.
      2.   The class will be divided into small groups of four to six.
      3.   The instructor will provide a handout or visual presentation of the individual descriptions presented below under "D. Instructions to Students."
      4.   The groups will be asked to discuss the possible sources of power for each scenario.   Each group should select a representative to take notes summarizing the group's findings that he or she will report to the entire class.
      5.   After 15 to 20 minutes, the small groups will be asked to terminate their discussions and participate in a full-class discussion.
      6.   A representative from each group will be asked to share her or his summary of the discussion. Comments will be encouraged from others.

D.   **Instructions for Students**
      1.   Sources of power include:
            -    information
            -    wealth
            -    reputation

---

[1] See Council on Social Work Education (CSWE) Educational Policy and Accreditation Standards (EPAS) Educational Policy (EP) 2.1.7, ("Apply knowledge of human behavior and the social environment").

- high status
- decision-making positions
- laws and policies
- connections

2.   Discuss the possible sources of power for the following individuals:

   a.   A newspaper editor who has a gambling problem and is in great debt.
   b.   The wealthy CEO (Chief Executive Officer) of a multimillion dollar business that manufactures tractors and other farm equipment.
   c.   The middle-class town board chairperson of Flab City, Nebraska.
   d.   The only priest at a rural Roman Catholic church.
   e.   A wealthy, popular talk show host.
   f.   A famous, highly skilled, and popular football player.
   g.   The neighborhood gossip.
   h.   The President of the United States
   i.   The chief director of the FBI.
   j.   The high school homecoming queen and cheerleader.
   k.   The president of the local League of Women Voters chapter.
   l.   The Chancellor or President of your college or university.
   m.   A local police officer.
   n.   You.

+---+
| **Competencies/Practice Behaviors Exercise 10.2** |
| **Community Empowerment for an Individual** |
+---+

Focus Competencies or Practice Behaviors:
- EP 2.1.3a   Distinguish, appraise, and integrate multiple sources of knowledge, including research-based knowledge and practice wisdom
- EP 2.1.4a   Recognize the extent to which a culture's structures and values may oppress, marginalize, alienate, or create or enhance privilege and power
- EP 2.1.7b   Critique and apply knowledge to understand person and environment
- EP 2.1.10e Assess client strengths and limitations

A.   **Brief Description**
You will respond to a vignette describing an older adult resident by assessing actual and potential sources of power and proposing means of community empowerment.

B.   Objectives

You will:

1.   "Recognize how diversity characterizes and shapes the human experience" for older adults.[2]

2.   "Critique and apply knowledge to understand person and environment" concerning the sources of power for an older adult community resident.[3]

3.   Propose means by which the community might empower this resident.

C.   Procedure

1.   Review the content on people and power in communities, social support networks, and empowerment and communities.

2.   Read the vignette below under "D. Instructions for Students."

3.   A full-class discussion will focus on the ensuing questions.

D.   Instructions for Students

Read the scenario below and answer the subsequent questions:

SCENARIO: A concerned neighbor, Al, referred Chuck, 77, to the Hustlebustle County Older Adults Protective Services Unit. Chuck lives in his small rundown two-story home in an urban neighborhood. Al reported that twice he found Chuck had fallen helplessly on the ground while walking out to get his mail. Both times Al had to practically carry Chuck back into the house. Chuck has rheumatoid arthritis which makes it very difficult to walk even with his two canes. Additionally, his eyesight is very poor. Al also raised questions about Chuck's ability to shop and cook for himself.

Chuck's wife Vicki died two years ago after a long bout with intestinal cancer. Since her death, Chuck has remained isolated and alone. He has three sons. Only his oldest son Mike, 48, lives in the area 12 miles away and owns a small delicatessen. Mike works long hours to keep his business afloat and has little time to spend with his own family, let alone with Chuck. Mike and his wife Jane have three teenage daughters. Chuck is proud of his grandchildren and looks forward to seeing them on holidays. Jane works part-time in the deli to help out whenever she can. Jane calls Chuck every few weeks to see how he's doing. Sometimes, she drives him to medical appointments or to pick up some groceries.

Chuck's second son Horace, 42, is a pop artist in San Francisco. The youngest, Henry, 35, is a worm farmer in Idaho. Both are single. Chuck usually talks to them on the phone every month or two.

Chuck used to attend church regularly. However, the church is located four blocks from his home and he finds it too difficult to walk there. He no longer can drive.

---

[2] See EPAS EP 2.1.4 ("Engage diversity and difference in practice").

[3] See EPAS EP 2.1.7.

Chuck considers himself an intelligent, independent man who worked hard all of his life as a carpenter. However, since his arthritis took a turn for the worse ten years ago, he has had to stop working. He is now facing financial difficulties. He has experienced many years of little income and high health costs for both he and his wife. He is becoming increasingly depressed at his failing health. However, he clings doggedly to the notion he must remain in his home. To do otherwise, he thinks to himself, would mean giving up and accepting certain death. Chuck is aware of the Happy Heavenly Health Care Center, a nursing home five blocks from his home. He has sadly watched some of his friends enter it and dreads the thought of having to go himself.

In summary, Chuck's problems include: failing health involving arthritis, poor eyesight, and intestinal distress (the last of which he does not like to talk about); loneliness; having few activities to keep him busy; and feeling unwanted and unimportant. Strengths include: intelligence; independence; ownership of his home; having concerned children; and an outgoing, sociable personality. Some of Chuck's likes include: a love of reading classical novels (on bright days when his eyesight improves slightly); seeing his children; playing stud poker; and drinking beer (not light, because he thinks it tastes like colored water).

1. In what ways does Chuck have power and in what ways does he not? (Power may involve information, wealth, reputation, high status, holding a decision-making position, laws and policies, connections.)
2. What social support networks might be developed or enhanced for Chuck to empower him?
3. In what other ways might Chuck's involvement with the community be enhanced?

Competencies/Practice Behaviors Exercise 10.3
Community Assessment for Empowerment

Focus Competencies or Practice Behaviors:
- EP 2.1.3a   Distinguish, appraise, and integrate multiple sources of knowledge, including research-based knowledge and practice wisdom
- EP 2.1.7b   Critique and apply knowledge to understand person and environment
- EP 2.1.9a   Continuously discover, appraise, and attend to changing locales, populations, scientific and technological developments, and emerging societal trends to provide relevant services
- EP 2.1.10a   Substantively and affectively prepare for action with individuals, families, groups, organizations, and communities

A.   Brief Description
You are given a take-home assignment focusing on the analysis of community strengths in your home or campus community.

B.   Objectives
You will:
1.   "Critique and apply knowledge to understand person and environment" by examining the strengths and weaknesses inherent in a community.[4]
2.   Evaluate the extent to which the community empowers its residents.
3.   Use critical thinking to "distinguish, appraise, and integrate multiple sources of knowledge" concerning your own communities.[5]

C.   Procedure
1.   Review the material on the 12 dimensions of community assessment.
2.   Research these dimensions either in your home community or the community in which the campus is located, and write up the results as a paper assignment. A community must be assessed for its strengths and weaknesses before approaches for empowerment can be implemented.

D.   Instructions for Students
Focus on either your home community or the community in which the campus is located, and respond to the following questions. If it's too difficult to obtain such information for an entire community, you may focus on a community neighborhood with which you are familiar. Many questions are based on the 11 dimensions of community assessment proposed by Sheafor and Horejsi (2012; pp. 169-170).

1.   *Demographics.*
- What are the community's boundaries and basic demographic characteristics (Netting, Kettner, & McMurtry, 2012; Rubin & Rubin, 2008; Sheafor & Horejsi, 2012)?
- What is the *population size* (the total number of persons living in a designated community), *density* (the ratio of people living within a particular space), and *heterogeneity* (the extent to which community members have diverse characteristics)?
- What ethnic groups live in the community?
- Do these ethnic groups speak languages other than English?
- Identify the names given to various parts of the community. Are different areas known for having their own characteristics? For example, if it's a larger community, is there an industrial area with several factories?
- Are there some neighborhoods characterized by blue-collar families and others by wealthy professionals and business people?
- Does one section have a university with its accompanying academic and student populations and activities?
- Where is the community located with respect to other communities, towns, and cities?

---

[4] See EPAS EP 2.1.7.
[5] See EPAS EP 2.1.3 ("Apply critical thinking to inform and communicate professional judgments").

- Is it relatively isolated or close to other communities that could provide resources and services?
- Identify the names given to various parts of the community. Are different areas known for having their own characteristics? For example, if it's a larger community, is there an industrial area with several factories?
- What is the area's history?
- How old is the community?
- How has it developed over time?
- What changes have occurred regarding who has populated the area?
- Have certain groups moved away and others moved in? If so, why?

2. *Geography and environmental influences on community.*
- What kind of environment encompasses the community (Rubin & Rubin, 2008)?
- Is it in the middle of the central prairies, connected by interstate highways with other communities at great distances?
- Is it located on an ocean, major river, or one of the Great Lakes where shipping and boating are primary economic and recreational activities, respectfully?
- Is it located in the mountains where winter might cause transportation difficulties?
- Are there recreational areas such as parks available?
- To what extent is the community experiencing environmental hazards like pollution, smog, or tainted water, or deprivations like power shortages?

3. *Beliefs and attitudes.*
- What are the "cultural values, traditions, and beliefs" that matter to various segments of the population (Netting et al., 2012, p. 205)?
- What are the spiritual and political values of the various factions of community residents?
- What social service agencies are available in the community and how do residents receive and value them?
- To what extent do residents feel an integral and supported part of the community? Or do they feel isolated and alone?

4. *Local politics.*
- How is the government structured? For example, cities, towns, and counties can be structured quite differently in terms of who has decision-making power and control.
- Are there any major issues currently under debate? For example, residents might have conflicting views regarding paying for a new middle school or rezoning a residential area to a business one.

5. *Local economy and businesses.*
   - What businesses, factories, and other sources of employment characterize the community?
   - Is the local economy thriving or in a major slump?
   - Are businesses owned by local residents or huge conglomerates based in other states?
   - What kinds of jobs exist in the community?
   - Do people work inside the community or simply live there and work somewhere else?
   - Is there adequate public transportation for people to get to and from work?
   - What is the unemployment rate?

6. *Income distribution.*
   - To what extent do community residents receive cash and in-kind (goods and services) public assistance benefits?
   - What are the median income levels for men, women, and various ethnic groups?
   - What percentage of people live in poverty?

7. *Housing.*
   - What are housing conditions like in the community?
   - Is it a relatively new community with low population density? Or it is an aging, economically deprived community with a high population density and deteriorating, dilapidated housing?
   - What are the "types of housing" characterizing the area ("for example, single-family dwellings, apartments, public housing") (Sheafor & Horejsi, 2012, p. 169)?
   - What are average rents and costs for real estate?
   - Is there a shortage of low-income housing?

8. *Educational facilities and programs.*
   Context:
   - What is the educational system like?
   - Are schools well supported by the community, or are they experiencing funding cut after funding cut?
   - Where and in what types of neighborhoods are schools located?
   - Are they public, private, or charter schools?

   Treatment of Special Populations of Children:
   - How are children with special needs treated?
   - To what extent are programs available for preschool children to prepare them for school entry? For instance, are Headstart programs available?
   - Are there diagnostic and treatment services available for children who have developmental disabilities?
   - Are schools perceptive regarding the ethnic and cultural makeup of their students?
   - Do they celebrate or discourage diversity?

138

Extent to which the School System Enables Students To Do Well:

- How do children typically score on standardized achievement tests compared to other communities in the U. S. and Canada?
- How well do community students compete with students from other communities in events such as science fairs, spelling competitions, and other contests?
- How well prepared for high school and college are students?
- How many students graduate and go on to college?
- Does elementary school provide them with a solid foundation for future levels of higher education, vocational education, and job training?
- What is the school drop-out rate?

The Community Educational System's Attention to Adult Residents:

- To what extent do parents understand their children's development?
- How well do community educational programs adequately prepare adults to enter the labor force?

9.   *Health and welfare systems.*

- Are there adequate numbers of health professionals and specialists?
- Are hospitals and clinics readily accessible to area residents?
- Are residents adequately covered by private insurance or public programs?
- To what extent is attention given to "the prevention and treatment of those conditions that afflict inner-city and poor people of color at disproportionate rates" (Naparstek & Dooley, 1997, p. 84)?
- What social service programs are available and where are they located?
- What specific types of services exist (for example, crisis intervention, substance abuse treatment, and public assistance)?
- How accessible and well-publicized are these programs?
- To what extent are they adequate, or are there substantial gaps in service?
- To what extent do service providers respect the needs and values of minority populations?
- If the community has non-English-speaking residents, are translators available?
- Are "self-help groups and informal helping networks" available in the community (Sheafor & Horejsi, 2012, p. 170)?
- To what extent are fire and police protection adequate?
- To what extent is the environment safe?
- Are housing standards and codes being followed?
- Are the public safety and justice systems sensitive to the needs and issues faced by minorities in the community?

10. *Sources of information and public opinion.*
    - Are there "influential TV and radio stations and newspapers to which the people look for information and perspectives on current events" (Sheafor & Horejsi, 2012, p. 170)?
    - How do community residents find out about what's happening in their community, state, nation, and the world?
    - Are there neighborhood organizations or other active community groups whose purposes are to keep on top of what's going on within the community? For example, are residents aware that commercial developers are planning to build a toxic waste plant in the near vicinity? Do residents know that school classroom populations have climbed to a ratio of one teacher for 45 students? Do community members know about a job training program subsidized by the County and targeting people in need?
    - To what extent does the community have human resources? (*Human resources* are the knowledge and abilities characterizing some people that can be used to enhance other people's quality of life [Barker, 2003]).
    - Are there significant community political, religious, or other informal community leaders who speak for various subgroups and minorities in the population and to whom people look for help and support?

11. *Summary assessment of community issues.*
    - What is your overall assessment of the community's functioning?
    - To what extent is it good or inadequate?
    - What serious social problems (for example, "inadequate housing, inadequate public transportation, insufficient law enforcement, lack of jobs, youth gangs, poverty, teen pregnancy, domestic abuse") do community residents face (Sheafor & Horejsi, 2012, p. 170)?
    - What primary "gaps" are evident in "social, health care, and educational services" (Sheafor & Horejsi, 2012, p. 170)?
    - To what extent and in what ways do you feel that the community empowers its residents?

Competencies/Practice Behaviors Exercise 10.4
Community Building and Professional Ethics

Focus Competencies or Practice Behaviors:
- EP 2.1.2b Make ethical decisions by applying standards of the National Association of Social Workers Code of Ethics and, as applicable, of the International Federation of Social Workers/International Association of Schools of Social Work Ethics in Social Work, Statement of Principles
- EP 2.1.7b Critique and apply knowledge to understand person and environment

- EP 2.1.9a   Continuously discover, appraise, and attend to changing locales, populations, scientific and technological developments, and emerging societal trends to provide relevant services
- EP 2.1.10a   Substantively and affectively prepare for action with individuals, families, groups, organizations, and communities

A.   Brief Description

A full-class discussion addresses the extent to which community building in all its facets complies with professional ethics.

B.   Objectives

You will:

1.   "Apply strategies of ethical reasoning to arrive at principled decisions" concerning the ethics of community building.[6]

2.   "Make ethical decisions by applying standards of the National Association of Social Workers Code of Ethics."[7]

C.   Procedure

1.   Review the content on community building and the basic values inherent in the *NASW Code of Ethics* (the latter of which are portrayed in the box below).

The six core values in the *NASW Code of Ethics* include (NASW, 1999):

1.   *Service:*   Providing help, resources, and benefits so that people may achieve their maximum potential.

2.   *Social justice:* Upholding the condition that in a perfect world, all citizens would have identical "rights, protection, opportunities, obligations, and social benefits" regardless of their backgrounds and membership in diverse groups (Barker, 2003, pp. 404-405).

3.   *Dignity and worth of the person:* Holding in high esteem and appreciating individual value.

4.   *Importance of human relationships:*   Valuing the dynamic reciprocal interactions between social workers and clients, including how they communicate, think and feel about each other, and behave toward each other.

5.   *Integrity:* Maintaining trustworthiness and sound adherence to moral ideals.

6.   *Competence:*   Having the necessary skills and abilities to perform work with clients effectively.

---

[6] See EPAS EP 2.1.2 ("Apply social work ethical principles to guide professional practice").
[7] See EPAS EP 2.1.2.

2. A full-class discussion will address the following question.
To what extent does the concept of community building comply with these principles? Explain in what ways.

Competencies/Practice Behaviors Exercise 10.5
Macro Practice Roles

Focus Competencies or Practice Behaviors:
- EP 2.1.1c   Attend to professional roles and boundaries
- EP 2.1.5b   Advocate for human rights and social and economic justice
- EP 2.1.5c   Engage in practices that advance social and economic justice
- EP 2.1.7b   Critique and apply knowledge to understand person and environment
- EP 2.1.8a   Analyze, formulate, and advocate for policies that advance social well-being
- EP 2.1.8b   Collaborate with colleagues and clients for effective policy action
- EP 2.1.9a   Continuously discover, appraise, and attend to changing locales, populations, scientific and technological developments, and emerging societal trends to provide relevant services
- EP 2.1.9b   Provide leadership in promoting sustainable changes in service delivery and practice to improve the quality of social services
- EP 2.1.10a   Substantively and affectively prepare for action with individuals, families, groups, organizations, and communities
- EP 2.1.10h   Initiate actions to achieve organizational goals
- EP 2.1.10j   Help clients resolve problems
- EP 2.1.10k   Negotiate, mediate, and advocate for clients

A. **Brief Description**
   You will assess a range of social work practice situations and propose the appropriate macro practice roles that can be used in each.

B. **Objectives**
   You will:
   1. Describe a range of social work roles in macro practice.
   2. Examine the significance of each role in a social work practice situation.

C. **Procedure**
   1. Review the material below on social work roles in macro practice.
   2. The class will be divided into small groups of four to six.
   3. The groups will be asked to identify the appropriate potential social work roles in macro practice for each vignette.
   4. After about 20 minutes, the small groups will be asked to terminate their discussions and participate in a full-class discussion.

---

5.   A representative from each group will be asked to share her or his summary of the discussion. Comments will be encouraged from all class members.

D.   **Instructions for Students**
1.   Review the following content on roles social workers can assume in macro practice.

> ### Social Worker Roles in Macro Practice
>
> Generalist social work practitioners may assume a *wide range of professional roles* in macro practice. A *role* is a culturally expected behavior pattern for a person having a specified status or being involved in a designated social relationship. For example, people have certain expectations of how social workers will act and of the activities they will pursue.
>
> Professional roles in macro practice include enabler, mediator, coordinator, manager, educator, evaluator, broker, facilitator, initiator, negotiator, mobilizer, and advocate. Note that professional roles are not necessarily mutually exclusive. A worker may perform the functions of more than one role at a time. Similarly, aspects of the roles may overlap.
>
> An *enabler* provides support, encouragement, and suggestions to members of a macro client system, thus allowing the system to operate more easily and more successfully in completing tasks and/or solving problems. In the enabler role, a worker helps a client system become capable of coping with situational or transitional stress. Specific skills used in achieving this objective include conveying hope, reducing resistance and ambivalence, recognizing and managing feelings, identifying and supporting personal strengths and social assets, breaking down problems into parts that can more readily be solved [partialization], and maintaining a focus on goals and the means of achieving them (Barker, 2003). For example, an enabler might help a community develop a program for identifying and shutting down crack houses. Community citizens do the work, but the enabler provides enthusiastic encouragement and helps participants identify their strengths and weaknesses and work out their interpersonal conflicts while keeping on task. Enablers, then, are helpers. Practitioners can function in the role of enabler for systems of all sizes.
>
> (Note that this definition of enabler is very different from that used in the topic area of substance abuse. There, the term refers to someone else such as a family member or friend who facilitates the substance abuser in continuing to use and abuse the drug of his or her choice.

143

A *mediator* resolves arguments or disagreements among micro, mezzo, and/or macro systems in conflict (Toseland & Rivas, 2012). At the macro level mediators help various factions (subsystems) in a community or community systems themselves work out their differences. For example, a community (or neighborhood) and a social services organization may require mediation over the placement of a substance abuse treatment center. Perhaps the social services organization has selected a prime spot, but the community or neighborhood is balking at the establishment of such a center within its boundaries.

The social worker may have to improve communication among dissident individuals or groups, or help those involved arrive at a compromise. A mediator remains neutral, not siding with either party in the dispute. Mediators strive to understand the positions of both parties. They may help to clarify positions, recognize miscommunication about differences, and help those involved present their cases clearly.

Coordination involves bringing components together in some kind of organized manner. A *coordinator*, therefore, brings the people involved in various systems together and organizes their performance (Netting et al., 2012; Yessian & Broskowski, 1983). A generalist social worker can function as a coordinator in many contexts including synchronization of advocacy pursuits, social service projects, the lobbying of legislators for some policy change, the provision of specialized consultation, or the process of enhancing the linkages between clients and services.

A *manager* in social work is one who assumes some level of administrative responsibility for a social services agency or some other organizational system (Burghardt, 2011; Kettner, Moroney, & Martin, 2013). Management involves the "attainment of organizational goals in an efficient and effective manner through planning, organizing, leading, and controlling organizational resources" (Daft & Marcic, 2013, p. 9).

An *educator* gives information and teaches skills to other systems. To be an effective educator, the worker must be knowledgeable about the topics being taught and a good communicator so that information is conveyed clearly.

An *evaluator* determines the extent to which a program or agency is effective (Brody, 2005; Kettner et al., 2013). This can occur in an organizational or community context. Generalist social workers with a broad knowledge base about systems of all sizes can analyze or evaluate how well programs and systems work. Likewise, they can evaluate the effectiveness of their own interventions with individuals, groups, organizations, and communities.

A *broker* links the macro client system (individuals, groups, organizations, or communities) with community resources and services. Such resources might be financial, legal, educational, psychological, recreational, or health-oriented.

A *facilitator* is one who guides a group experience. Although the facilitator role is very common in mezzo practice, workers also frequently assume it in macro practice. In the macro context a facilitator brings participants together to promote the change process by improving communication, helping direct their efforts and resources, and linking them with needed information and expert help.

An ***initiator*** is the person or persons who call attention to an issue. The issue in the community may be a problem, a need, or simply a situation that can be improved. It is important to recognize that a problem does not have to exist before a situation can be dealt with. Often preventing future problems or enhancing existing services is a satisfactory reason for creating a change effort. Thus, a social worker may recognize that a policy has the potential to create problems for particular clients and bring this to the attention of her supervisor. Likewise, a client may identify ways that service could be improved. In each case, the worker is playing the role of initiator in terms of beginning the actual change process. Usually, this role must be followed up by other kinds of work, because merely pointing out problems does not guarantee they will be solved.

A ***negotiator*** is an intermediary who acts to settle disputes and/or resolve disagreements. However, unlike mediators, negotiators clearly take the side of one of the parties involved.

A ***mobilizer*** identifies and convenes community people and resources and makes them responsive to unmet community needs (Austin, 2008; Toseland & Rivas, 2012). The mobilizer's purpose is to match resources to needs in the community context. Sometimes, a mobilizer's goal involves making services more accessible to those in the community who need them. Other times, a goal is initiating and developing services to meet needs that heretofore were unmet.

Advocacy is active intervention on a client system's behalf to get needed resources that are currently unavailable, or to change regulations or policies that negatively affect that client system. An ***advocate*** is one who steps forward and speaks out on behalf of the client system in order to promote fair and equitable treatment or gain needed resources. In macro practice, of course, it would be on the behalf of some macro client system. This may be especially appropriate when a macro client system has little power to get what it needs. It also often involves taking risks, especially when advocating on a client's behalf in the face of a larger, more powerful system.

2.   Identify the Macro Practice Role(s) assumed in the following case scenarios. As indicated above, the potential roles include **enabler, mediator, coordinator, manager, educator, evaluator, broker, facilitator, initiator, negotiator, mobilizer,** and **advocate.** Note that in some scenarios the worker may play more than one role. Explain how each role functions in the scenario.

A. A social worker employed by a neighborhood center determines that the various workers and other professionals dealing with adolescent clients are not communicating with each other. (A *neighborhood center* is a locally-based facility intending to bring neighborhood residents together by providing services, resources, and opportunities for interaction.) For example, school social workers have no established procedure for conveying information to protective services workers who, in turn, do not communicate readily with probation and parole workers—despite the fact that these professionals are working with many of the same clients. The neighborhood center social worker decides to bring together representatives from the various agencies that serve the center and establish more clearly defined communication channels.

Macro Practice Role(s):

Explanation:

B. A worker in a Child Protective Services Unit has developed special skills in family counseling by participating in a two-year training program. Her agency's Assistant Director asks her to provide a series of six in-service training program for other Child Protective Services staff. *(In-service training programs* are educational sessions provided by an agency for its staff to develop their skills or improve their effectiveness.)

Macro Practice Role(s):

Explanation:

C. The main tasks of a Foster Care Unit are to assess potential foster parent applicants, monitor placement, manage cases as children move in and out of foster care, and train foster parents in parenting and behavior-management skills. The unit social workers hold biweekly meetings to discuss how to improve agency service provision. The workers take turns organizing the meetings and running the discussions.

Macro Practice Role(s):

Explanation:

D. A social worker employed by a large private family services agency specializes in international adoptions, especially those involving countries from Northeastern Europe, Central Asia, and China. He discovers that many of the adoptive children suffer from health problems caused by early nutritional deprivation. The worker is convinced that this is not a matter of one or two problem cases, but a disturbing pattern. No automatic referral process is in place to assess these adoptive children and direct their families to needed resources, including designated medical specialists. The worker devises a systematic process for assessment and referral.

Macro Practice Role(s):

Explanation:

E. Agency administration asks one of three social workers in a large residential health care complex for older adults to assess the effectiveness of its social services program.

Macro Practice Role(s):

Explanation:

F. A social worker employed at a sheltered workshop for people with intellectual disabilities is assigned by her supervisor to oversee a new program that will teach anger management and appropriate assertiveness skills to clients. *(Sheltered employment* such as this workshop for people with intellectual disabilities is a program involving work in a safe, closely supervised work environment for people who have trouble functioning more independently.) The social worker will also be responsible for supervising two other social workers and training them to implement the program with their clients.

Macro Practice Role(s):

Explanation:

147

G. A group of clients inform their social worker that the community is trying to enforce a housing maintenance ordinance in a punitive and excessively picky manner. Enforcers have been sent to these clients' homes and have cited them for such minuscule matters as having pieces of siding that need repainting and rusted rain gutters. These clients are poor and have almost no access to resources for anything other than basic necessities. They implore their social worker to help them. She learns that the original intent of the ordinance was to ascertain the safety of the clients' living conditions: Were steps and railings broken? Were windows broken? Had lead paint been used? The worker, therefore, judges that both the client group and the community are trying to do the best they can, so she attempts to referee the dispute between the community client group and the community leaders imposing the ordinance.

Macro Practice Role(s):

Explanation:

H. A social worker employed by a large public social services department increasingly hears client complaints about drug houses popping up in their residential neighborhoods. The worker identifies clients and other concerned citizens, and organizes a community meeting. He then assists community residents in formulating a plan to identify drug house locations and establish a procedure for reporting such houses to the authorities.

Macro Practice Role(s):

Explanation:

I. A social worker at a public assistance agency is terribly troubled by the conditions in the clients' waiting room and by the tedious process of client intakes. She explores the issue, develops a proposed plan for improvement, and makes an appointment to speak with the agency's executive director about it.

Macro Practice Role(s):

Explanation:

J. A local charitable organization cuts off its contribution to a Planned Parenthood agency with a large, centrally located main clinic and three satellite clinics. *(Planned Parenthood* agencies assist people in making decisions about pregnancy and promote birth control and contraception.) The result will be a severe cutback in services and the closure of at least two satellite clinics. A huge number of clients will find it difficult if not impossible to receive adequate services. A social work counselor at one of the clinics, with the support of her supervisor, gathers facts to show the importance of the funding and arranges a meeting with the funding organization's leaders. She hopes to discuss the cuts and persuade the charitable agency to reverse its decision.

Macro Practice Role(s):

Explanation:

K. A juvenile probation officer is distressed by proposed legislation that will shut down a vocational training program for juvenile offenders because of its expense. He talks to other workers and administrators in his state agency, and gathers facts and statistics that demonstrate the program's cost effectiveness. He then calls and writes to influential legislators, and meets with the chairperson of the legislative committee that recommended closing the program. He also contacts other concerned social workers and encourages them to join his effort.

Macro Practice Role(s):

Explanation:

L. A group of community residents approaches a social worker to ask about starting a Neighborhood Watch program. *(Neighborhood Watch Programs* are locally based crime prevention programs where neighborhood residents volunteer to keep a careful lookout for each other in order to watch out for and stop crime.) The worker provides them with encouragement and information.

Macro Practice Role(s):

Explanation:

REFERENCES

Austin, D. M. (2008). The human service executive. In J. Rothman, J. L. Erlich, & J. E. Tropman (Eds.), *Strategies of community intervention* (7th ed., pp. 269-385). Peosta, IA: Eddie Bowers.

Barker, R. L. (2003). *The social work dictionary* (5th ed.). Washington, DC: NASW Press.

Burghardt, S. (2011). *Macro practice in social work for the 21st century*. Thousand Oaks, CA: Sage.

Council on Social Work Education (CSWE). (2008). *Educational policy and accreditation standards (EPAS)*. Alexandria, VA: Author. (Available at www.cswe.org.)

Daft, R. L., & Marcic, D. (2013). *Understanding management* (8th ed.). Mason, OH: South-Western.

Kettner, P. M., Moroney, R. M., & Martin, L. L. (2013). *Designing and managing programs: An effectiveness-based approach* (4th ed.). Thousand Oaks, CA: Sage.

Naparstek, R. J., & Dooley, D. (1997). Community building. *In Encyclopedia of social work supplement* (19th ed., pp. 77-89). Washington, DC: NASW Press.

National Association of Social Workers (NASW). (1999). *Code of ethics*. Washington, DC: Author.

Netting, F. E., Kettner, P. M., & McMurtry, S. (2012). *Social work macro practice* (5th ed.). Boston: Allyn & Bacon.

Rubin, H. J., & Rubin, I. S. (2008). *Community organizing and development* (4th ed.). Boston: Allyn & Bacon.

Sheafor, B. W., & Horejsi, C. R. (2012). *Techniques and guidelines for social work practice* (9th ed.). Boston: Allyn & Bacon.

Toseland, R. W., & Rivas, R. F. (2012). *An introduction to group work practice* (7th ed.). Boston: Allyn & Bacon.

Yessian, M. R., & Broskowski, A. (1983). Generalists in human service systems: Their problems and prospects. In R. M. Kramer & H. Specht (Eds.), *Readings in community organization practice* (pp. 180–198). Englewood Cliffs, NJ: Prentice-Hall.

Chapter 10 Competencies/Practice Behaviors Exercises Assessment:

Name: _____ **Date:** _____

Supervisor's Name: _____

Focus Competencies/Practice Behaviors:

- EP 2.1.1c   Attend to professional roles and boundaries
- EP 2.1.2b   Make ethical decisions by applying standards of the National Association of Social Workers Code of Ethics and, as applicable, of the International Federation of Social Workers/International Association of Schools of Social Work Ethics in Social Work, Statement of Principles
- EP 2.1.3a   Distinguish, appraise, and integrate multiple sources of knowledge, including research-based knowledge and practice wisdom
- EP 2.1.4a   Recognize the extent to which a culture's structures and values may oppress, marginalize, alienate, or create or enhance privilege and power
- EP 2.1.5b   Advocate for human rights and social and economic justice
- EP 2.1.5c   Engage in practices that advance social and economic justice
- EP 2.1.7b   Critique and apply knowledge to understand person and environment
- EP 2.1.8a   Analyze, formulate, and advocate for policies that advance social well-being
- EP 2.1.8b   Collaborate with colleagues and clients for effective policy action
- EP 2.1.9a   Continuously discover, appraise, and attend to changing locales, populations, scientific and technological developments, and emerging societal trends to provide relevant services
- EP 2.1.9b   Provide leadership in promoting sustainable changes in service delivery and practice to improve the quality of social services
- EP 2.1.10a   Substantively and affectively prepare for action with individuals, families, groups, organizations, and communities
- EP 2.1.10e   Assess client strengths and limitations
- EP 2.1.10h   Initiate actions to achieve organizational goals
- EP 2.1.10j   Help clients resolve problems
- EP 2.1.10k   Negotiate, mediate, and advocate for clients

Instructions:

A.   Evaluate your work or your partner's work in the Focus Competencies/Practice Behaviors by completing the Competencies/Practice Behaviors Assessment form below

B.   What other Competencies/Practice Behaviors did you use to complete these Exercises? Be sure to record them in your assessments

1.	I have attained this competency/practice behavior (in the range of 81 to 100%)							
2.	I have largely attained this competency/practice behavior (in the range of 61 to 80%)							
3.	I have partially attained this competency/practice behavior (in the range of 41 to 60%)							
4.	I have made a little progress in attaining this competency/practice behavior (in the range of 21 to 40%)							
5.	I have made almost no progress in attaining this competency/practice behavior (in the range of 0 to 20%)							

EPAS 2008 Core Competencies & Core Practice Behaviors	Student Self Assessment						Evaluator Feedback
Student and Evaluator Assessment Scale and Comments	0	1	2	3	4	5	Agree/Disagree /Comments
EP 2.1.1 Identify as a Professional Social Worker and Conduct Oneself Accordingly:							
a. Advocate for client access to the services of social work							
b. Practice personal reflection and self-correction to assure continual professional development							
c. Attend to professional roles and boundaries							
d. Demonstrate professional demeanor in behavior, appearance, and communication							
e. Engage in career-long learning							
f. Use supervision and consultation							
EP 2.1.2 Apply Social Work Ethical Principles to Guide Professional Practice:							
a. Recognize and manage personal values in a way that allows professional values to guide practice							
b. Make ethical decisions by applying NASW Code of Ethics and, as applicable, of the IFSW/IASSW Ethics in Social Work, Statement of Principles							
c. Tolerate ambiguity in resolving ethical conflicts							
d. Apply strategies of ethical reasoning to arrive at principled decisions							
EP 2.1.3 Apply Critical Thinking to Inform and Communicate Professional Judgments:							
a. Distinguish, appraise, and integrate multiple sources of knowledge, including research-based knowledge and practice wisdom							
b. Analyze models of assessment, prevention, intervention, and evaluation							
c. Demonstrate effective oral and written communication in working with individuals, families, groups, organizations, communities, and colleagues							
EP 2.1.4 Engage Diversity and Difference in Practice:							
a. Recognize the extent to which a culture's structures and values may oppress, marginalize, alienate, or create or enhance privilege and power							
b. Gain sufficient self-awareness to eliminate the influence of personal biases and values in working with diverse groups							
c. Recognize and communicate their understanding of the importance of difference in shaping life experiences							
d. View themselves as learners and engage those with whom they work as informants							

EP 2.1.5 Advance Human Rights and Social and Economic Justice:							
a. Understand forms and mechanisms of oppression and discrimination							
b. Advocate for human rights and social and economic justice							
c. Engage in practices that advance social and economic justice							
EP 2.1.6 Engage in Research-Informed Practice and Practice-Informed Research:							
a. Use practice experience to inform scientific inquiry							
b. Use research evidence to inform practice							
EP 2.1.7 Apply Knowledge of Human Behavior and the Social Environment:							
a. Utilize conceptual frameworks to guide the processes of assessment, intervention, and evaluation							
b. Critique and apply knowledge to understand person and environment							
EP 2.1.8 Engage in Policy Practice to Advance Social and Economic Well-Being and to Deliver Effective Social Work Services:							
a. Analyze, formulate, and advocate for policies that advance social well-being							
b. Collaborate with colleagues and clients for effective policy action							
EP 2.1.9 Respond to Contexts that Shape Practice:							
a. Continuously discover, appraise, and attend to changing locales, populations, scientific and technological developments, and emerging societal trends to provide relevant services							
b. Provide leadership in promoting sustainable changes in service delivery and practice to improve the quality of social services							
EP 2.1.10 Engage, Assess, Intervene, and Evaluate with Individuals, Families, Groups, Organizations and Communities:							
a. Substantively and affectively prepare for action with individuals, families, groups, organizations, and communities							
b. Use empathy and other interpersonal skills							
c. Develop a mutually agreed-on focus of work and desired outcomes							
d. Collect, organize, and interpret client data							
e. Assess client strengths and limitations							
f. Develop mutually agreed-on intervention goals and objectives							
g. Select appropriate intervention strategies							
h. Initiate actions to achieve organizational goals							
i. Implement prevention interventions that enhance client capacities							
j. Help clients resolve problems							
k. Negotiate, mediate, and advocate for clients							
l. Facilitate transitions and endings							
m. Critically analyze, monitor, and evaluate interventions							

Chapter 11
Neighborhood Empowerment

Competencies/Practice Behaviors Exercise 11.1
Identifying and Comparing Types of Neighborhoods

Focus Competencies or Practice Behaviors:
- EP 2.1.7b   Critique and apply knowledge to understand person and environment
- EP 2.1.10a   Substantively and affectively prepare for action with individuals, families, groups, organizations, and communities

A.   **Brief Description**
You will match types of neighborhoods with their respective definitions.

B.   **Objectives**
You will:
1.   Identify various types of neighborhoods.
2.   Explore the neighborhood as one of "the range of social systems in which people live."[1]

C.   **Procedure**
1.   You will be provided with copies of the matching exercise under "D. Instructions for Students."
2.   You will be allowed a few minutes to complete the exercise, after which the instructor will initiate a discussion with the class regarding major similarities and differences among these types of neighborhoods.

D.   **Instructions for Students**
Match the following types of neighborhoods with their respective definitions:

1.	Stepping-Stone	_____
2.	Transitory	_____
3.	Diffuse	_____
4.	Integral	_____
5.	Anomic	_____
6.	Parochial	_____

---

[1] See Council on Social Work Education (CSWE) *Educational Policy and Accreditation Standards (EPAS)* Educational Policy (EP) 2.1.7, ("Apply knowledge of human behavior and the social environment").

a.   A neighborhood with residents who live there temporarily and who have little access to resources and are probably not moving up in the world.

b.   A neighborhood that offers residents a strong sense of neighborhood identification and often strong linkages with the larger community, but little social interaction with each other.

c.   A neighborhood where residents are highly involved with each other, readily identify themselves as part of the neighborhood, and feel clearly linked with the encompassing larger community.

d.   A neighborhood that is high on interaction and identification but low on community connections.

e.   A neighborhood where residents live there temporarily because they are moving up in their careers and possibly starting and raising families; residents may positively identify themselves with the neighborhood, yet have low levels of commitment to interact with other residents or to work on the neighborhood's behalf.

f.   A neighborhood that is dysfunctional and provides little social support; residents tend to live in these neighborhoods for long periods of time, yet feel little identification with other residents.

Competencies/Practice Behaviors Exercise 11.2
You and Your 'Hood

Focus Competencies or Practice Behaviors:
- EP 2.1.1b   Practice personal reflection and self-correction to assure continual professional development
- EP 2.1.7b   Critique and apply knowledge to understand person and environment

A.   Brief Description
You will form small groups, describe your neighborhoods of origin, and assess what type of neighborhood it is.

B.   Objectives
You will:
1.   Describe your neighborhood of origin.
2.   Investigate your own neighborhood as one of "the range of social systems in which people live."[2]

C.   Procedure
1.   Review the material on: functions of neighborhoods; describing neighborhood structure; and neighborhoods, ethnicity, and social class.
2.   The class will be divided into small groups of four to six.

---

[2] See *EPAS* EP 2.1.7.

3. The groups will be asked to discuss the questions posed below under "D. Instructions for Students." Each group should select a representative to take notes summarizing the group's findings that she or he will share with the entire class.

4. After about 10 minutes, the small groups will be asked to terminate their discussions and participate in a full-class discussion.

5. A representative from each group will be asked to share her or his summary of the discussion. Comments will be encouraged from others.

D. Instructions for Students

Each group member should answer and then discuss the following questions:

1. How would you describe your neighborhood? Cite at least three adjectives.

2. To what extent does your neighborhood fit into one of the categories for types of neighborhoods (integral, parochial, diffuse, stepping-stone, transitory, or anomic)? Explain why.

Competencies/Practice Behaviors Exercise 11.3
Analyzing Positive Neighborhood Functions

Focus Competencies or Practice Behaviors:

- EP 2.1.3a   Distinguish, appraise, and integrate multiple sources of knowledge, including research-based knowledge and practice wisdom
- EP 2.1.7b   Critique and apply knowledge to understand person and environment
- EP 2.1.10a Substantively and affectively prepare for action with individuals, families, groups, organizations, and communities

A. Brief Description

You are presented with a series of vignettes illustrating how a neighborhood might empower its residents. You are then asked to discuss which neighborhood functions are involved in each vignette.

B. Objectives

You will:

1. Appraise a range of vignettes concerning how neighborhoods as "social systems promote or deter people in maintaining or achieving health and well-being."[3]

2. Apply critical thinking by discussing which positive, empowering functions of neighborhoods apply to each vignette.[4]

---

[3] See *EPAS* EP 2.1.7.

[4] See *EPAS* EP 2.1.3 ("Apply critical thinking to inform and communicate professional judgments").

C. Procedure

1. Review the material on the five functions of neighborhoods and the qualities of strong neighborhoods in terms of promoting optimal health and well-being.
2. The instructor will read the vignettes presented below under "D. Instructions for Students" and initiate a discussion for each regarding which functions the vignettes indicate are being fulfilled and how.

D. Instructions for Students

For each of the following vignettes (Kretzmann and McKnight, 1993), discuss which of the five functions of neighborhoods are being fulfilled and describe the qualities that make them strong. (Note that more than one function may be involved for any one vignette.) The five functions of neighborhoods are:

1. Provision of an arena for social interaction.
2. Provision of mutual aid.
3. Provision of an arena for people to communicate and share information.
4. Provision of opportunities for people to congregate with other people having similar status, cultural backgrounds, or interests as themselves (Rubin & Rubin, 2008).
5. Provision of an organizational and political base.

Vignette A: Residents in a public housing project identified unemployment as a major problem. They banded together and formulated job training sessions that addressed issues like developing resumes, preparing and dressing for interviews, answering questions asked during job interviews, emphasizing personal strengths, and establishing good work habits. Additionally, they developed a system for identifying job openings and referring residents to them for full- and part-time employment.

Vignette B: A group of neighborhood residents living in a small town determined that they needed a place to hold community events. Thus, they established a reception center in a local church basement. They used the space for a wide range of local festivities including organizational banquets, fundraising festivities, neighborhood meetings, church events, and family reunions.

Vignette C: A neighborhood center's members became concerned about teens having little to do when school was out. The neighborhood had virtually no places for young people to congregate other than in alleys or on storefront sidewalks. The center's members rented a deserted warehouse and volunteered time to fix it up and make it into a recreational center. They also volunteered time to coach youth and supervise activities. In addition, they organized interested young people into a work club that emphasized identifying skills and finding part-time employment.

Vignette D: One neighborhood center identified homebound older adult residents' need for help plowing snow in winter and spading gardens in preparation for spring planting. Center members identified volunteers willing to participate in a mutual help program. Volunteers who did the physical labor for the older adults were called "The Earthmovers"; in return, older adults receiving help prayed for volunteers' well-being and were called "The Prayer Warriors" (p. 135). Each group's intent was to help the other.

Vignette E: Residents of a suburban neighborhood concluded that they needed greater communication among themselves about community events and each other's activities. There was no local paper except one in the nearby big city, so they got little detail about issues, activities, concerns, and accomplishments in their smaller community. Few residents had ready access to computers. Starting a newsletter, *The Community Chitchatter,* a group of volunteer residents visited door-to-door soliciting subscriptions and approaching local businesses for financial backing to help with initial start-up costs. A local school allowed the group to use space for evening meetings. Volunteers formed an editorial staff that solicited news items and articles. Once the newsletter became known, neighborhood residents sent in dozens of news items. The volunteer staff was able to publish and distribute the newsletter for minimal cost.

Vignette F: Community residents in St. Louis addressed the problems of teen pregnancy and school dropout by establishing the Teen Outreach Program (TOP) in 1978 (McDonald, 1998; NCSET, 2005). During one recent school year TOP served over 13,000 young people in 16 states throughout the country (NCSET, 2005). Weekly classes are offered either as part of the school curriculum or after school where participants "discuss topics such as communication skills, dealing with family stress, parenting, and understanding self and values"; volunteer experience such as "working as aides in hospitals and nursing homes, peer tutoring, and volunteer work in schools" is also required (NCSET, 2005). The program's strategy is that "the best way to help teenage girls avoid becoming pregnant is to involve them in voluntary activity, whether or not it is explicitly designed to point out the pitfalls of early parenthood" (McDonald, 1998, p. 48). TOP aims to reinforce members' self-esteem and change the way they view the world. It emphasizes participants' role in the community and the importance of caring for both others and themselves. One study found that TOP members were 40 percent less likely to become pregnant compared with a control group; other studies found decreased school dropout and suspension rates (NCSET, 2005). (Note that this does not mean that sex education is unimportant. TOP concepts mentioned here involving values, decision-making, and communication are important dimensions of effective sex education programs.)

Vignette G: Local chapter members of the National Association of Black Accountants volunteered time to help community residents and local businesses. They assisted with business start-ups, budget development, and other accounting tasks.

Competencies/Practice Behaviors Exercise 11.4
Critical Thinking about Conceptual Frameworks

Focus Competencies or Practice Behaviors:
- EP 2.1.3a   Distinguish, appraise, and integrate multiple sources of knowledge, including research-based knowledge and practice wisdom
- EP 2.1.7a   Utilize conceptual frameworks to guide the processes of assessment, intervention, and evaluation
- EP 2.1.7b   Critique and apply knowledge to understand person and environment

A.   **Brief Description**
In small groups, apply critical thinking skills to compare and contrast the strengths and weaknesses of two conceptual frameworks describing neighborhood structure.

B.   **Objectives**
You will:
1.   Apply critical thinking to appraise two conceptual frameworks describing neighborhood structure.[5]
2.   Assess strengths and weaknesses characterizing these frameworks.

C.   **Procedure**
1.   Review the content regarding the two conceptual frameworks describing neighborhood structure. The first concerns interpersonal interaction, identification, and connections. The second relates to neighborhood groups and value implementation.
2.   You will form small groups of four to six.
3.   You will be asked to discuss the questions posed below under "D. Instructions for Students." Each group should select a representative to take notes summarizing the group's findings that she or he will share with the entire class.
4.   After about 10 minutes, the small groups will be asked to terminate their discussions and participate in a full-class discussion.
5.   A representative from each group will be asked to share her or his summary of the discussion. Comments will be encouraged from others.

---

[5] See *EPAS* EP 2.1.3.

D.   Instructions for Students

Your instructor will review the material on conceptual frameworks describing neighborhood structure. The class will then be broken down into small groups. Discuss the following questions:

1.   What are the strengths and weaknesses of the two conceptual frameworks describing neighborhood structure—the first emphasizing interpersonal interaction, identification, and connections, and the second focusing on neighborhood groups and value implementation?

2.   In what ways might each framework help a social worker conceptualize the macro social environment to enhance his or her ability to practice in it?

REFERENCES

Council on Social Work Education (CSWE). (2008). *Educational policy and accreditation standards (EPAS)*. Alexandria, VA: Author. (Available at www.cswe.org.)

Kretzmann, J. P., & McKnight, J. L. (1993). *Building communities from the inside out: A path toward finding and mobilizing a community's assets.* Chicago, IL: ACTA Publications.

McDonald, M. (1998, January 5). How to reduce teen pregnancy: Voluntary community service. *U.S. New & World Report,* 48-49.

National Center on Secondary Education and Transition (NCSET). (2005). Part III: What works in dropout prevention. Retrieved on May 16, 2009 from http://www.ncset.org/publications/essentialtools/dropout/part3.3.11.asp .

Rubin, H. J., & Rubin, I. S. (2008). *Community organizing and development* (4th ed.). Boston: Allyn & Bacon.

Chapter 11 Competencies/Practice Behaviors Exercises Assessment:

Name: _____ **Date:** _____

Supervisor's Name: _____

Focus Competencies/Practice Behaviors:
- EP 2.1.1b   Practice personal reflection and self-correction to assure continual professional development
- EP 2.1.3a   Distinguish, appraise, and integrate multiple sources of knowledge, including research-based knowledge and practice wisdom
- EP 2.1.7a   Utilize conceptual frameworks to guide the processes of assessment, intervention, and evaluation
- EP 2.1.7b   Critique and apply knowledge to understand person and environment
- EP 2.1.10a   Substantively and affectively prepare for action with individuals, families, groups, organizations, and communities

Instructions:

A.   Evaluate your work or your partner's work in the Focus Competencies/Practice Behaviors by completing the Competencies/Practice Behaviors Assessment form below

B.   What other Competencies/Practice Behaviors did you use to complete these Exercises? Be sure to record them in your assessments

1.	I have attained this competency/practice behavior (in the range of 81 to 100%)
2.	I have largely attained this competency/practice behavior (in the range of 61 to 80%)
3.	I have partially attained this competency/practice behavior (in the range of 41 to 60%)
4.	I have made a little progress in attaining this competency/practice behavior (in the range of 21 to 40%)
5.	I have made almost no progress in attaining this competency/practice behavior (in the range of 0 to 20%)

EPAS 2008 Core Competencies & Core Practice Behaviors	Student Self Assessment						Evaluator Feedback
Student and Evaluator Assessment Scale and Comments	0	1	2	3	4	5	Agree/Disagree/ Comments
EP 2.1.1 Identify as a Professional Social Worker and Conduct Oneself Accordingly:							
a. Advocate for client access to the services of social work							
b. Practice personal reflection and self-correction to assure continual professional development							
c. Attend to professional roles and boundaries							
d. Demonstrate professional demeanor in behavior, appearance, and communication							
e. Engage in career-long learning							
f. Use supervision and consultation							

EP 2.1.2 Apply Social Work Ethical Principles to Guide Professional Practice:								
a.	Recognize and manage personal values in a way that allows professional values to guide practice							
b.	Make ethical decisions by applying NASW Code of Ethics and, as applicable, of the IFSW/IASSW Ethics in Social Work, Statement of Principles							
c.	Tolerate ambiguity in resolving ethical conflicts							
d.	Apply strategies of ethical reasoning to arrive at principled decisions							
EP 2.1.3 Apply Critical Thinking to Inform and Communicate Professional Judgments:								
a.	Distinguish, appraise, and integrate multiple sources of knowledge, including research-based knowledge and practice wisdom							
b.	Analyze models of assessment, prevention, intervention, and evaluation							
c.	Demonstrate effective oral and written communication in working with individuals, families, groups, organizations, communities, and colleagues							
EP 2.1.4 Engage Diversity and Difference in Practice:								
a.	Recognize the extent to which a culture's structures and values may oppress, marginalize, alienate, or create or enhance privilege and power							
b.	Gain sufficient self-awareness to eliminate the influence of personal biases and values in working with diverse groups							
c.	Recognize and communicate their understanding of the importance of difference in shaping life experiences							
d.	View themselves as learners and engage those with whom they work as informants							
EP 2.1.5 Advance Human Rights and Social and Economic Justice:								
a.	Understand forms and mechanisms of oppression and discrimination							
b.	Advocate for human rights and social and economic justice							
c.	Engage in practices that advance social and economic justice							
EP 2.1.6 Engage in Research-Informed Practice and Practice-Informed Research:								
a.	Use practice experience to inform scientific inquiry							
b.	Use research evidence to inform practice							
EP 2.1.7 Apply Knowledge of Human Behavior and the Social Environment:								
a.	Utilize conceptual frameworks to guide the processes of assessment, intervention, and evaluation							
b.	Critique and apply knowledge to understand person and environment							
EP 2.1.8 Engage in Policy Practice to Advance Social and Economic Well-Being and to Deliver Effective Social Work Services:								
a.	Analyze, formulate, and advocate for policies that advance social well-being							
b.	Collaborate with colleagues and clients for effective policy action							

EP 2.1.9 Respond to Contexts that Shape Practice:							
a.	Continuously discover, appraise, and attend to changing locales, populations, scientific and technological developments, and emerging societal trends to provide relevant services						
b.	Provide leadership in promoting sustainable changes in service delivery and practice to improve the quality of social services						
EP 2.1.10 Engage, Assess, Intervene, and Evaluate with Individuals, Families, Groups, Organizations and Communities:							
a.	Substantively and affectively prepare for action with individuals, families, groups, organizations, and communities						
b.	Use empathy and other interpersonal skills						
c.	Develop a mutually agreed-on focus of work and desired outcomes						
d.	Collect, organize, and interpret client data						
e.	Assess client strengths and limitations						
f.	Develop mutually agreed-on intervention goals and objectives						
g.	Select appropriate intervention strategies						
h.	Initiate actions to achieve organizational goals						
i.	Implement prevention interventions that enhance client capacities						
j.	Help clients resolve problems						
k.	Negotiate, mediate, and advocate for clients						
l.	Facilitate transitions and endings						
m.	Critically analyze, monitor, and evaluate interventions						

Chapter 12
Diversity, Populations-at-Risk, and Empowerment in the Macro Social Environment

---

Competencies/Practice Behaviors Exercise 12.1
Community Empowerment through Groups—African American Grandparents

Focus Competencies or Practice Behaviors:
- EP 2.1.4   Engage diversity and difference in practice
- EP 2.1.4a   Recognize the extent to which a culture's structures and values may oppress, marginalize, alienate, or create or enhance privilege and power
- EP 2.1.4c   Recognize and communicate their understanding of the importance of difference in shaping life experiences
- EP 2.1.5a   Understand forms and mechanisms of oppression and discrimination
- EP 2.1.5b   Advocate for human rights and social and economic justice
- EP 2.1.5c   Engage in practices that advance social and economic justice
- EP 2.1.7   Apply knowledge of human behavior and the social environment
- EP 2.1.7b   Critique and apply knowledge to understand person and environment
- EP 2.1.8a   Analyze, formulate, and advocate for policies that advance social well-being
- EP 2.1.8b   Collaborate with colleagues and clients for effective policy action
- EP 2.1.9a   Continuously discover, appraise, and attend to changing locales, populations, scientific and technological developments, and emerging societal trends to provide relevant services

A. **Brief Description**

You will examine a case vignette involving African American grandparents and discuss how the establishment of groups provided empowerment.

B. **Objectives**

You will:

1. "Critique and apply knowledge to understand person and environment" by focusing on a segment of the African American population.[1]

2. "Understand how diversity characterizes and shapes the human experience" for this African American population.[2]

---

[1] See Council on Social Work Education (CSWE) *Educational Policy and Accreditation Standards (EPAS)* Educational Policy (EP) 2.1.7, ("Apply knowledge of human behavior and the social environment") and EPAS EP 2.1.4 ("Engage diversity and difference in practice").

[2] See *EPAS* EP 2.1.4.

3.   Examine a case example reflecting community and group empowerment.
4.   Identify specific means by which group empowerment was used "to promote … people in maintaining or achieving health and well-being."[3]

C.   Procedure
1.   Review the material on social action groups and empowerment in chapter four.
2.   The instructor will read the case example presented below.
3.   A full-class discussion will be conducted concerning how the vignette demonstrates the five means of group empowerment cited below.

D.   Instructions for Students
1.   Focus on the following case example:

CASE EXAMPLE: Okazawa-Rey (1998) provides an example of a community response to the needs of African American grandparents who have become primary caretakers of their grandchildren. The initiating problem is one well established in the community and national scenes. Many people have become addicted to crack-cocaine and are relinquishing their responsibilities as parents and productive citizens to pursue drug use. An example of a program responding to this problem is the Grandparents Who Care Support Network of San Francisco. Most members are "poor and working class, middle-aged and elderly African-American women" (Cox, 2002; Okazawa-Rey, 1998, p. 54). They have gained custody of their grandchildren because of their own children's neglect. This is due to drug abuse, incarceration because of drug convictions, and the unwillingness to submit their grandchildren to strangers in the public foster care system.

These grandparents have found themselves in the strange and unusual circumstance of having sudden responsibility for small children at a stage in life when they feel they were done with all that. This problem is compounded with the health problems many children suffer due to poor prenatal care, drug use during pregnancy, and child neglect. These grandparents "desperately need day care, special education services, transportation, respite care, and money" (Okazawa-Rey, 1998, p. 54). To get services, they find themselves trying to negotiate the confusing maze of bureaucracies governing service provision.

Two health care workers, Doriane Miller and Sue Trupin, identified the problems and needs, and established Grandparents Who Care (Okazawa-Rey, 1998). The program is based on four philosophical principles. First, individual health problems transcend the fault of the individual. They are related to mezzo and macro conditions. Second, cultural, legal, and organizational barriers often hinder access to needed services. Third, even if people can get needed services, they may be inadequate and unable to meet needs. Fourth, empowerment at the micro, mezzo, and macro levels is necessary for maintaining optimal health and well-being (Breidenstein, 2003).

---

[3] See *EPAS* EP 2.1.7.

Grandparents Who Care established a series of support groups to provide information, emotional support, and practical advice. Groups consist of two to twenty-five grandparents, are co-led by professional health care personnel including nurses or social workers, and meet weekly for 90 minutes. Grandparents Who Care has a board of directors made up of grandparents, citizens, and concerned health care professionals who advise the organization.

Group members provide each other with support and help addressing a range of issues. For example, "When one woman faces a particular problem with her grandchild in the school system, another one will describe her dealings with this system and offer suggestions concerning the most effective ways to intercede" (Okazawa-Rey, 1998, p. 58). Members can thus share their experiences with each other and help work through issues. The professional co-leaders can assist the group by providing technical information about service availability, eligibility, and accessibility.

Grandparents Who Care expanded its work in several macro dimensions to further empower its members. First, grandparents were trained as group leaders who go out and form new groups. In this way, the program's supportive help spread to help grandparents elsewhere in the community.

Second, Grandparents Who Care undertook political advocacy and lobbying on its members' behalf. One problem advocates addressed involved the legal difficulties grandparents experienced in receiving foster care payments. As relatives, they did not technically qualify as foster parents. Other financial support available to them was not nearly as good as that provided to unrelated foster parents. Grandparents Who Care advocates lobbied with a state legislator to pass a bill allowing grandparents to receive greater benefits.

2.   Describe and discuss in what ways this program seeks to achieve each of the following means of group empowerment:
    a.   Increasing understanding.
    b.   Inspiring others.
    c.   Consciousness raising.
    d.   Providing mutual support.
    e.   Using cooperation.

Competencies/Practice Behaviors Exercise 12.2
Analyzing Community Empowerment—Puerto Rican Grocery Stores

Focus Competencies or Practice Behaviors:
- EP 2.1.3a   Distinguish, appraise, and integrate multiple sources of knowledge, including research-based knowledge and practice wisdom
- EP 2.1.4   Engage diversity and difference in practice
- EP 2.1.4a   Recognize the extent to which a culture's structures and values may oppress, marginalize, alienate, or create or enhance privilege and power

- EP 2.1.4c   Recognize and communicate their understanding of the importance of difference in shaping life experiences
- EP 2.1.5b   Advocate for human rights and social and economic justice
- EP 2.1.7   Apply knowledge of human behavior and the social environment
- EP 2.1.7b   Critique and apply knowledge to understand person and environment

A.   Brief Description
The class is divided into small groups to discuss how a case example reflects various means of community empowerment.

B.   Objectives
You will:
1.   Examine a case example reflecting community empowerment.
2.   "Critique and apply knowledge to understand person and environment" by focusing on a segment of the Puerto Rican community.[4]
3.   "Understand how diversity characterizes and shapes the human experience" for this Puerto Rican population.[5]
4.   Identify specific means by which community empowerment was used "to promote … people in maintaining or achieving health and well-being."[6]

C.   Procedure
1.   Review the material on people and power in communities, citizen participation, social support networks, and empowerment in communities in chapter 10.
2.   You will form small groups of four to six.
3.   The instructor will read the case example presented below.
4.   The groups will be asked to discuss as instructed below, select a group representative, and be prepared to report to the entire class the small group's findings.
5.   After about 15 minutes, the small groups will be asked to terminate their discussions and participate in a full-class discussion.
6.   A representative from each group will be asked to share her or his summary of the discussion. Comments will be encouraged from others in the class.

D.   Instructions for Students
1.   One study of Puerto Rican owned grocery stores and restaurants found that such small businesses can serve their communities far beyond selling food (Delgado, 1996). They can:
    - Furnish credit and cash checks when necessary.
    - Provide information about community issues and events.
    - Supply information about what's going on in their homeland.
    - Provide informal counseling to people in crisis.

---

[4] See *EPAS* EP 2.1.7 and EP 2.1.4.
[5] See *EPAS* EP 2.1.4.
[6] See *EPAS* EP 2.1.7.

> ➢ Furnish information about relevant, available social services.
> ➢ Help community residents interpret and fill out government forms.
> ➢ Provide "cultural connectedness to the homeland through the selling of videotapes, publications," etc. (Delgado, 1997, p. 447).

2. Describe and discuss in what ways these activities seek to achieve personal and social empowerment for community residents.

Competencies/Practice Behaviors Exercise 12.3
Community Empowerment through Groups—Political Action Organizations on Behalf of Gay, Lesbian, Bisexual, Transgender, and Questioning People (GLBTQ)

Focus Competencies or Practice Behaviors:
- EP 2.1.3a   Distinguish, appraise, and integrate multiple sources of knowledge, including research-based knowledge and practice wisdom
- EP 2.1.4   Engage diversity and difference in practice
- EP 2.1.4a   Recognize the extent to which a culture's structures and values may oppress, marginalize, alienate, or create or enhance privilege and power
- EP 2.1.4c   Recognize and communicate their understanding of the importance of difference in shaping life experiences
- EP 2.1.5a   Understand forms and mechanisms of oppression and discrimination
- EP 2.1.5b   Advocate for human rights and social and economic justice
- EP 2.1.5c   Engage in practices that advance social and economic justice
- EP 2.1.7   Apply knowledge of human behavior and the social environment
- EP 2.1.7b   Critique and apply knowledge to understand person and environment
- EP 2.1.10k Negotiate, mediate, and advocate for clients

A.   **Brief Description**
     Students examine a discussion about political action organizations and discuss how such an organization can empower GLBTQ people.

B.   **Objectives**
     You will:
     1. "Critique and apply knowledge to understand person and environment" by focusing on the rights of the GLBTQ population.[7]
     2. "Understand how diversity characterizes and shapes the human experience" for the GLBTQ population.[8]
     3. Identify and assess specific means by which political action organizations may empower GLBTQ people to help them maintain or achieve "health and well-being."[9]

---

[7] See *EPAS* EP 2.1.7 and EP 2.1.4.
[8] See *EPAS* EP 2.1.4.

C.   Procedure

     1.   Review the material on social action groups and empowerment in chapter four.

     2.   The class will be divided into small groups of four to six.

     3.   The instructor will read the case example presented below.

     4.   The groups will be asked to discuss as instructed below, select a group representative, and be prepared to report to the entire class the small group's findings.

     5.   After about 15 minutes, the small groups will be asked to terminate their discussions and participate in a full-class discussion.

     6.   A representative from each group will be asked to share her or his summary of the discussion. Comments will be encouraged from others in the class.

D.   Instructions for Students

     1.   Focus on the following discussion of some of the activities performed by political action organizations:

POLITICAL ACTION ORGANIZATIONS

    A *political action organization* is based on the concept of a social action group. It is an organization that conducts "coordinated efforts to influence legislation, election of candidates, and social causes" (Barker, 2003, p. 330). Changing legislation and social policy on the behalf of GLBTQ people can involve the provision of due and equal rights, the purging of discrimination, and the enhancement of overall well-being.

    Political action organizations working on the behalf of GLBTQ (gay, lesbian, bisexual, transgender, and questioning) people can function in at least three ways (Barker, 2003). These include providing direct support to political candidates, educating the public to gain support, and conducting legislative advocacy (Barker, 2003, Messinger, 2006).

    Supporting Political Candidates. Political action organizations can attend to several facets of this process. First, they must explore and determine a particular candidate's position on the issues. Questions can be posed about the candidate's ideology and prior behavior. To what extent did the candidate support GLBTQ rights in the past? What are the candidate's verbal stance and/or voting record on such issues as anti-hate legislation and gay marriage?

---

[9] See *EPAS* EP 2.1.7.

Second, because political campaigns cost money, a primary means of supporting political candidates is through financial support. This is often done by forming and working through a *political action committee (PAC),* a group whose purpose is to raise money and provide support for designated political candidates (Barker, 2003; Haynes & Mickelson, 2003). PACs may be formed within a political action organization or in an organization pursuing a broader range of goals than solely political action. A PAC can participate in any number of fund-raising activities, from bake sales to walk-a-thons to direct solicitation for financial support.

Third, political action organizations can also provide candidates support by endorsing them. The "PAC can endorse the candidate by stating that the membership organization (for example, the NASW [National Association of Social Workers]) recommends that social workers vote for that candidate" (Haynes & Mickelson, 2003, p. 158). Haynes and Mickelson (2003) elaborate:

"Services and support can be offered, including mailing and telephone lists. Candidates are aware that the endorsement alone will not guarantee membership votes, but mailing lists and telephone numbers facilitate the candidate's ability to reach PAC members and to gain their support and labor. . . . A PAC can recruit and assign volunteers from its membership to assist candidates, thereby increasing the effect of the endorsement" (p. 159).

Educating the Public to Gain Support. A political action organization can work to influence public opinion to enlighten citizens about GLBTQ issues and mobilize citizens to vote on GLBTQ people's behalf. Citizens support politicians who, in turn, formulate laws that govern our macro social environment. Social workers can urge voters to critically think about issues of self-determination and expand their perceptions about human rights with respect to GLBTQ people.

In order to educate effectively, it's first important to define the issues and know the relevant facts (Hoefer, 2006). Myths and stereotypes that support prejudice against gay and lesbian people must be identified and disputed (Morrow, 2006).

Conducting Legislative Advocacy. *Advocacy* is the practice of actively intervening on the behalf of clients so that they get what they need (Kirst-Ashman & Hull, 2012). *Legislative advocacy* is the process of influencing legislators to support legislation promoting specific goals. *Lobbying* is the practice of seeking "direct access to lawmakers to influence legislation and public policy"; the expression originated when people seeking to influence lawmakers met with them in the lobbies of legislative houses (Barker, 2003, p. 253). Political organizational members can lobby legislators or testify before legislative committees to educate decision makers about issues and encourage them to vote in GLBTQ people's best interest. The same principles involved in the earlier discussion concerning educating the general public also apply here.

> *Case Example.* An example of a political action organization activity is to establish a statewide telephone network where members contact designated other members who in turn would initiate their own designated telephone contacts and so on. Before legislative decisions are made, members can alert each other to the issues via the network. Members can then exert immediate pressure upon legislative decision makers by writing letters, emailing, or phoning in their pleas advocating for whatever GLBTQ rights issue had current legislative attention.

2. Describe and discuss the ways in which a political action organization may most effectively seek to achieve each of the following means of empowerment for GLBTQ people:
    a. Increasing understanding.
    b. Inspiring others.
    c. Consciousness-raising.
    d. Providing mutual support.
    e. Using cooperation.

Competencies/Practice Behaviors Exercise 12.4
Community Empowerment for Pregnant Women

Focus Competencies or Practice Behaviors:
- EP 2.1.3a Distinguish, appraise, and integrate multiple sources of knowledge, including research-based knowledge and practice wisdom
- EP 2.1.4 Engage diversity and difference in practice
- EP 2.1.4c Recognize and communicate their understanding of the importance of difference in shaping life experiences
- EP 2.1.5c Engage in practices that advance social and economic justice
- EP 2.1.7 Apply knowledge of human behavior and the social environment
- EP 2.1.7a Utilize conceptual frameworks to guide the processes of assessment, intervention, and evaluation
- EP 2.1.7b Critique and apply knowledge to understand person and environment
- EP 2.1.10g Select appropriate intervention strategies
- EP 2.1.10h Initiate actions to achieve organizational goals
- EP 2.1.10i Implement prevention interventions that enhance client capacities
- EP 2.1.10j Help clients resolve problems

A. **Brief Description**
You will examine a case vignette and discuss how a community empowered pregnant women by providing prenatal care.

B. **Objectives**
You will:
1. Use a feminist conceptual framework to assess the human experience of a population of pregnant women.[10]
2. "Understand how diversity characterizes and shapes the human experience" for this population of pregnant women.[11]
3. Assess how the macro community system might "promote or deter people in maintaining or achieving health and well-being."[12]

C. **Procedure**
1. Review the material on empowerment in the macro environment for women in this chapter and that on feminist theories in chapter 3.
2. The class will be divided into small groups of four to six.
3. The instructor will read the case example presented below.
4. The groups will be asked to participate in a discussion as instructed below, select a group representative, and be prepared to report to the entire class the small group's findings.
5. After about 15 minutes, the small groups will be asked to terminate their discussions and participate in a full-class discussion.
6. A representative from each group will be asked to share her or his summary of the discussion. Comments will be encouraged from others in the class.

D. **Instructions for Students**
1. Read the following case example:

> *CASE EXAMPLE:* Shared Beginnings, a Denver program, provides a good example of how various facets of a community came together to address the issue of the importance of good prenatal care (Balsanek, 1998). Initial consciousness-raising occurred through extensive media coverage of the problem, alerting the public to the fact that increasing numbers of poor, single and young mothers failed to seek or receive prenatal care. The project was spearheaded by a concerned volunteer philanthropist who brought citizens, social services representatives, health care personnel, and potential financial backers together to initiate the project. Fundraising projects included a luncheon program supported by influential community members and solicitation of financial donations.

---

[10] See *EPAS* EP 2.1.7 and EP 2.1.4.
[11] See *EPAS* EP 2.1.4.
[12] See *EPAS* EP 2.1.7.

Participants involved in the project established five basic program goals. The first was to educate the community concerning the importance of prenatal health care and alter attitudes on health care's behalf. A second goal was the initiation of a "Sharing Partners" program where volunteer paraprofessionals would go out into the community to educate residents about prenatal care and encourage them to use services (p. 414). The third goal was to establish an ongoing agency complete with director, administrative assistant and volunteer coordinator to oversee progress. The fourth was the creation of a "Baby Store" located in a local hospital where "coupons could be redeemed for new baby care items to reinforce health care appointment attendance before the baby is born and immunizations after the baby is born" (p. 414). The final goal was to integrate a research component to evaluate the program's effectiveness and provide suggestions for improvement. In summary, "Shared Beginnings represents a grassroots approach to providing the community support that poor and at-risk families need to raise healthy children" (p. 418).

2. Describe in what ways, if any, participants sought to achieve each of the following means of empowerment:
   a. Using a gender filter.
   b. Assuming a pro-woman perspective.
   c. Empowerment.
   d. Consciousness-raising.
   e. Viewing personal issues as political concerns.
   f. Stressing the importance of process.
   g. Appreciating diversity as being as important as unity and harmony.
   h. Validation.

Competencies/Practice Behaviors Exercise 12.5
What Does Spirituality Mean to You?

Focus Competencies or Practice Behaviors:
- EP 2.1.1b   Practice personal reflection and self-correction to assure continual professional development
- EP 2.1.4   Engage diversity and difference in practice
- EP 2.1.4b   Gain sufficient self-awareness to eliminate the influence of personal biases and values in working with diverse groups
- EP 2.1.4c   Recognize and communicate their understanding of the importance of difference in shaping life experiences

A. **Brief Description**
   In small groups, you will discuss the Navajo community's spirituality, describe your own conception of spirituality, and compare the two.

B. **Objectives**
You will:
1. Explore the dimension of diversity involving older adult Navajo people in terms of spirituality in addition to divergent values and beliefs from those of the mainstream culture.[13]
2. Describe your own personal conception of spirituality to "gain self-awareness" with the goal of eliminating "the influence of personal biases and values."[14]
3. Compare and contrast their own conceptions of spirituality with that of the Navajo community.

C. **Procedure**
1. Review the material on the Navajo community, spirituality, and respect for older adult members.
2. The class will be divided into small groups of four to six.
3. You will be asked to discuss a number of questions concerning the Navajo and your personal conceptions of spirituality. There will be a full-class discussion following the small group discussions.
4. Before the groups begin, the instructor will read the instructions given below.
5. After about 20 minutes, the small groups will be asked to terminate their discussions and participate in a full-class discussion.

D. **Instructions for Students**
1. Summarize what each of the following six cultural dimensions means to the Navajo community in terms of its members' daily life and spirituality (Mercer, 1996, pp. 186-188):
   a. Communication.
   b. Clan associations and social structure.
   c. Personal space, modesty, privacy, and cleanliness.
   d. Traditional food.
   e. Dying and death.
   f. Cultural rituals.
2. Describe your own personal conception of spirituality.
3. Discuss how your own personal conception of spirituality is similar to or different from that of the Navajo.

---

[13] See *EPAS* EP 2.1.4.
[14] See *EPAS* EP 2.1.4.

Focus Competencies or Practice Behaviors:

- EP 2.1.3a   Distinguish, appraise, and integrate multiple sources of knowledge, including research-based knowledge and practice wisdom
- EP 2.1.4   Engage diversity and difference in practice
- EP 2.1.4a   Recognize the extent to which a culture's structures and values may oppress, marginalize, alienate, or create or enhance privilege and power
- EP 2.1.7   Apply knowledge of human behavior and the social environment
- EP 2.1.7b   Critique and apply knowledge to understand person and environment

A.   **Brief Description**

The class is broken down into small groups of four to six and provided discussion questions concerning a case vignette. The same client is viewed within the context of having four designated developmental disabilities. You will discuss how the social environment might better accommodate the client concerning each disability and its respective needs.

B.   **Objectives**

You will:

1.   Explore challenges in the social environment facing people with designated developmental disabilities and "recognize the extent to which a culture's structures and values may oppress" or "marginalize" this population.[15]

2.   Formulate ways in which social systems in the macro social environment can be made more accessible, thereby promoting these populations' "health and well-being."[16]

C.   **Procedure**

1.   Review the content on defining developmental disabilities.

2.   The instructor will read the following case scenario concerning Efra discussed below.

3.   The class will break into groups of four to six, and discuss the two questions noted below with respect to each of the four conditions cited. (Note that Efra should experience only one condition at a time.) At the end of about 20 minutes the groups will be asked to participate in a full-class discussion and share what they talked about. There should be a designated representative from each group.

---

[15] See *EPAS* EP 2.1.4.
[16] See *EPAS* EP 2.1.7.

4. After approximately 20 minutes, the instructor will terminate the small group discussions and ask students to participate in a full-class discussion.
5. A representative from each group will be asked to share her or his summary of the discussion and comments will be encouraged from others.

D. Instructions for Students

Read the following scenario and discuss the ensuing questions.

THE SCENARIO: Efra, age 22, has at least three tasks to accomplish on Wednesday. First, she must do her grocery shopping for the next week at the large Super Seller grocery store a few blocks from her home. Second, she must attend her college classes from 11:00 a.m. to 2:00 p.m. on the second floor of the Business Building at the College located three miles from her home. She does not have a car, so she must rely on public transportation or rides with friends. Third, she must get to her part-time job at Bogie's Burger Bonanza located about five blocks from her home. She is scheduled to work from 3:30 p.m. to 8:00 p.m.

Now, consider if Efra would have one of the developmental disabilities cited below. For each instance, discuss the following two questions:
1. *How would this condition affect Efra's ability to function?*
2. *How might her social environment be made more responsive to meet Efra's needs, making it easier for her to function and achieve her daily tasks?*

a. *Cerebral palsy:* (Efra can walk with crutches for short distances, but most often uses a motorized wheelchair when outside her apartment.)
b. *Seizure Disorder:* (Although Efra took medication, she typically had one to two seizures each day where she would suddenly "blank out" or lose consciousness for a period of two to seven minutes.)
c. *Hearing impairment:* (Efra cannot hear any sounds. She is adept at sign language and fairly good at reading lips if the person speaking faces her and enunciates clearly.)
d. *Visual impairment:* (Efra is legally blind, capable of discriminating only a slight difference between light and darkness.)
e. *Asperger syndrome:* (Efra has no significant delays in cognition and language, but does have difficulty communicating directly with others and forming interpersonal relationships.)

Focus Competencies or Practice Behaviors:

- EP 2.1.3a   Distinguish, appraise, and integrate multiple sources of knowledge, including research-based knowledge and practice wisdom
- EP 2.1.4   Engage diversity and difference in practice
- EP 2.1.4a   Recognize the extent to which a culture's structures and values may oppress, marginalize, alienate, or create or enhance privilege and power
- EP 2.1.4c   Recognize and communicate their understanding of the importance of difference in shaping life experiences
- EP 2.1.7b   Critique and apply knowledge to understand person and environment
- EP 2.1.10e   Assess client strengths and limitations
- EP 2.1.10g   Select appropriate intervention strategies
- EP 2.2   Generalist Practice

A.   **Brief Description**

You are asked to identify the means of empowerment used in a series of scenarios involving people with intellectual disabilities. You are also asked to formulate new ideas for empowering the people involved using alternative means of empowerment.

B.   **Objectives**

You will:

1.   "Assess client strengths and limitations" for several cases involving people with intellectual disabilities.[17]

2.   "Recognize the extent to which a culture's structures and values may oppress" people with intellectual disabilities.[18]

3.   Propose "appropriate intervention strategies"[19] to "build on the strengths and resiliency"[20] of people with intellectual disabilities for the purpose of their empowerment.

C.   **Procedure**

1.   Review content in the text concerning treatment of people with developmental disabilities and community empowerment for people with intellectual disabilities.

2.   The instructor will read the following vignettes and ask students to identify the means of empowerment used and to propose new strategies for building on people's strengths and resiliency.

---

[17] See *EPAS* 2.1.10(e).
[18] See *EPAS* 2.1.4 ("Engage diversity and difference in practice").
[19] See *EPAS* 2.1.10(g).
[20] See *EPAS* 2.2 ("Generalist Practice").

D.   Instructions for Students

For each of the following scenarios:

1.   Explain which means of empowerment (identified below) were used.
2.   Propose additional intervention strategies for empowerment.[21]

Means of empowerment include:

Information and referral service and help lines;
Provision of non-institutional living opportunities;
Vocational and employment opportunities;
Other support services;
Advocacy;
Using community volunteers;
Providing recreational activities.

Scenario #1:   Perry, 28, thrives at playing games. He lives at home with his parents and has little to do to fill up his time. Perry's neighbor acquainted him with the local Boys Club. He now volunteers there regularly, teaching children games and supervising their activities.

Scenario #2:   Felicita, 22, lives with her older sister and spends most weekdays at a day program with other people who have intellectual disabilities. She passes much of her time coloring and watching other residents. She is an exceptionally warm person who will light up with a dazzling smile when spoken to or given any attention. One of the day program staff introduced her to a local daycare center to see if she could help out there.

At first, the day program staff always accompanied her and provided some supervision. Now she goes to the daycare center by herself several times a week. The children love her and her attention. She always has time to listen to what they have to say and give them a hug when needed. They realize she's different than their other teachers because sometimes they have to help her out in completing activities. They don't care. They love her anyway.

---

[21] The following scenarios are loosely adapted from some portrayed in *Building Communities from the Inside Out* by J. P. Kretzmann and J. L. McKnight (Chicago: ACTA Publications, 1993).

Scenario #3:   Joe, 68, lives in a group home. He loves to bowl. Julietta, a member of the area's neighborhood association, stopped by one day to see if there was anything the association could do for Joe and the other residents. She found out about Joe's desire to bowl and remembered that a local church had a Thursday night bowling league. She talked to the team members and asked them if they would consider including Joe on their team. They were a bit hesitant as they took bowling very seriously and played desperately to win. They were even more hesitant when they discovered Joe was not a very good bowler. However, Joe obviously was ecstatic about being on the team. Team members worked out a rotation system where Joe could periodically bowl but his score was omitted from the final total. Joe continued to beam as he proudly wore his Beaver's Bowling Buddies T-shirt.

Scenario #4:   Norma, 35, is a pleasant, soft-spoken, shy woman who lives with her older adult parents. She and her parents would often shop at a small local drug store and gift shop across the street from their modest home.

Myrtle, who owned the store, got to know and like Norma and her family. Myrtle was concerned that Norma rarely got out of the house except for shopping and other errands with her parents. She started taking Norma out for lunch or a movie every other week or so. Although a busy businesswoman, Myrtle enjoys her time with Norma and feels Norma really appreciates it. She harbors some growing fears about what will happen to Norma when her parents die. Myrtle has become part of Norma's natural helping network.

REFERENCES

Balsanek, J. (1998). Addressing at-risk pregnant women's issues through community, individual, and corporate grassroots efforts. In P. L. Ewalt, E. M. Freemen, & D. L. Poole (Eds.), *Community building: Renewal, well-being, and shared responsibility* (pp. 411-419). Washington, DC: NASW Press.

Barker, R. L. (2003). *The social work dictionary.* Washington, DC: NASW Press.

Breidenstein, J. L. (2003). *The New Social Worker, 10* (2), 5-7.

Bricker-Jenkins, M., & Netting, F. E. (2009). Feminist issues and practices in social work. In A. R. Roberts (Editor-in-Chief), *Social workers' desk reference* (2nd ed., pp. 277-283). New York: Oxford.

Council on Social Work Education (CSWE). (2008). *Educational policy and accreditation standards (EPAS).* Alexandria, VA: Author. (Available at www.cswe.org.)

Cox, C. B. (2002). Empowering African American Custodial Grandparents. *Social Work, 47* (1), 45-54.

Delgado, M. (1996). Puerto Rican food establishments as social service organizations: Results of an asset assessment. *Journal of Community Practice, 3,* 57-77.

Delgado, M. (1997). Role of Latina-owned beauty parlors in a Latino community. *Social Work, 42* (5), 445-453.

Gutierrez, L. M., & Lewis, E. A. (1999). *Empowering women of color.* New York: Columbia.

Haynes, K. S., & Mickelson, J. S. (2003). *Affecting change: Social workers in the political arena* (5th ed.). Boston: Allyn & Bacon.

Hoefer, R. (2006). *Advocacy practice for social justice.* Chicago: Lyceum.

Kirst-Ashman, K. K., & Hull, G. H., Jr. (2012). *Understanding generalist practice* (6th ed.). Belmont, CA: Brooks/Cole.

Lee, J. A. B. (2001). *The empowerment approach to social work practice: Building the beloved community* (2nd. Ed.). New York: Columbia.

Mercer, S. O. (1996, March). Navajo elderly people in a reservation nursing home: Admission predictors and culture care practices. *Social Work, 41* (2), 181-189.

Messinger, L. (2006). Social welfare policy and advocacy. In D. F. Morrow & L. Messinger (Eds.), *Sexual orientation & gender expression in social work practice: Working with gay, lesbian, bisexual, & transgender people* (pp. 427-459). New York: Columbia University Press.

Morrow, D. F. (2006). Sexual orientation and gender identity expression. In D. F. Morrow & L. Messinger (Eds.), *Sexual orientation & gender expression in social work practice: Working with gay, lesbian, bisexual, & transgender people* (pp. 3-17). New York: Columbia University Press.

Okazawa-Rey, M. (1998). Empowering poor communities of color: A self-help model. In L. M. Gutierrez, R. J. Parsons, & E. O. Cox (Eds.) *Empowerment in social work practice: A sourcebook.* Pacific Grove, CA: Brooks/Cole.

Chapter 12 Competencies/Practice Behaviors Exercises Assessment:

Name: _____   **Date:** _____
Supervisor's Name: _____

Focus Competencies/Practice Behaviors:

- EP 2.1.1b   Practice personal reflection and self-correction to assure continual professional development
- EP 2.1.3a   Distinguish, appraise, and integrate multiple sources of knowledge, including research-based knowledge and practice wisdom
- EP 2.1.4   Engage diversity and difference in practice
- EP 2.1.4a   Recognize the extent to which a culture's structures and values may oppress, marginalize, alienate, or create or enhance privilege and power
- EP 2.1.4b   Gain sufficient self-awareness to eliminate the influence of personal biases and values in working with diverse groups
- EP 2.1.4c   Recognize and communicate their understanding of the importance of difference in shaping life experiences
- EP 2.1.5a   Understand forms and mechanisms of oppression and discrimination
- EP 2.1.5b   Advocate for human rights and social and economic justice
- EP 2.1.5c   Engage in practices that advance social and economic justice
- EP 2.1.7   Apply knowledge of human behavior and the social environment
- EP 2.1.7a   Utilize conceptual frameworks to guide the processes of assessment, intervention, and evaluation
- EP 2.1.7b   Critique and apply knowledge to understand person and environment
- EP 2.1.8a   Analyze, formulate, and advocate for policies that advance social well-being
- EP 2.1.8b   Collaborate with colleagues and clients for effective policy action
- EP 2.1.9a   Continuously discover, appraise, and attend to changing locales, populations, scientific and technological developments, and emerging societal trends to provide relevant services
- EP 2.1.10e   Assess client strengths and limitations
- EP 2.1.10g   Select appropriate intervention strategies
- EP 2.1.10h   Initiate actions to achieve organizational goals
- EP 2.1.10i   Implement prevention interventions that enhance client capacities
- EP 2.1.10j   Help clients resolve problems
- EP 2.1.10k   Negotiate, mediate, and advocate for clients
- EP 2.2   Generalist Practice

Instructions:

A.   Evaluate your work or your partner's work in the Focus Competencies/Practice Behaviors by completing the Competencies/Practice Behaviors Assessment form below
B.   What other Competencies/Practice Behaviors did you use to complete these Exercises? Be sure to record them in your assessments

1.	I have attained this competency/practice behavior (in the range of 81 to 100%)
2.	I have largely attained this competency/practice behavior (in the range of 61 to 80%)
3.	I have partially attained this competency/practice behavior (in the range of 41 to 60%)
4.	I have made a little progress in attaining this competency/practice behavior (in the range of 21 to 40%)
5.	I have made almost no progress in attaining this competency/practice behavior (in the range of 0 to 20%)

EPAS 2008 Core Competencies & Core Practice Behaviors	Student Self Assessment						Evaluator Feedback
Student and Evaluator Assessment Scale and Comments	0	1	2	3	4	5	Agree/Disagree/ Comments
EP 2.1.1 Identify as a Professional Social Worker and Conduct Oneself Accordingly:							
a. Advocate for client access to the services of social work							
b. Practice personal reflection and self-correction to assure continual professional development							
c. Attend to professional roles and boundaries							
d. Demonstrate professional demeanor in behavior, appearance, and communication							
e. Engage in career-long learning							
f. Use supervision and consultation							
EP 2.1.2 Apply Social Work Ethical Principles to Guide Professional Practice:							
a. Recognize and manage personal values in a way that allows professional values to guide practice							
b. Make ethical decisions by applying NASW Code of Ethics and, as applicable, of the IFSW/IASSW Ethics in Social Work, Statement of Principles							
c. Tolerate ambiguity in resolving ethical conflicts							
d. Apply strategies of ethical reasoning to arrive at principled decisions							
EP 2.1.3 Apply Critical Thinking to Inform and Communicate Professional Judgments:							
a. Distinguish, appraise, and integrate multiple sources of knowledge, including research-based knowledge and practice wisdom							
b. Analyze models of assessment, prevention, intervention, and evaluation							
c. Demonstrate effective oral and written communication in working with individuals, families, groups, organizations, communities, and colleagues							
EP 2.1.4 Engage Diversity and Difference in Practice:							
a. Recognize the extent to which a culture's structures and values may oppress, marginalize, alienate, or create or enhance privilege and power							
b. Gain sufficient self-awareness to eliminate the influence of personal biases and values in working with diverse groups							
c. Recognize and communicate their understanding of the importance of difference in shaping life experiences							
d. View themselves as learners and engage those with whom they work as informants							

EP 2.1.5 Advance Human Rights and Social and Economic Justice:								
a.	Understand forms and mechanisms of oppression and discrimination							
b.	Advocate for human rights and social and economic justice							
c.	Engage in practices that advance social and economic justice							
EP 2.1.6 Engage in Research-Informed Practice and Practice-Informed Research:								
a.	Use practice experience to inform scientific inquiry							
b.	Use research evidence to inform practice							
EP 2.1.7 Apply Knowledge of Human Behavior and the Social Environment:								
a.	Utilize conceptual frameworks to guide the processes of assessment, intervention, and evaluation							
b.	Critique and apply knowledge to understand person and environment							
EP 2.1.8 Engage in Policy Practice to Advance Social and Economic Well-Being and to Deliver Effective Social Work Services:								
a.	Analyze, formulate, and advocate for policies that advance social well-being							
b.	Collaborate with colleagues and clients for effective policy action							
EP 2.1.9 Respond to Contexts that Shape Practice:								
a.	Continuously discover, appraise, and attend to changing locales, populations, scientific and technological developments, and emerging societal trends to provide relevant services							
b.	Provide leadership in promoting sustainable changes in service delivery and practice to improve the quality of social services							
EP 2.1.10 Engage, Assess, Intervene, and Evaluate with Individuals, Families, Groups, Organizations and Communities:								
a.	Substantively and affectively prepare for action with individuals, families, groups, organizations, and communities							
b.	Use empathy and other interpersonal skills							
c.	Develop a mutually agreed-on focus of work and desired outcomes							
d.	Collect, organize, and interpret client data							
e.	Assess client strengths and limitations							
f.	Develop mutually agreed-on intervention goals and objectives							
g.	Select appropriate intervention strategies							
h.	Initiate actions to achieve organizational goals							
i.	Implement prevention interventions that enhance client capacities							
j.	Help clients resolve problems							
k.	Negotiate, mediate, and advocate for clients							
l.	Facilitate transitions and endings							
m.	Critically analyze, monitor, and evaluate interventions							

Chapter 13
Social Justice and the Global Community

Competencies/Practice Behaviors Exercise 13.1
Why Do Poverty and Inequality Exist?

Focus Competencies or Practice Behaviors:

- EP 2.1.1b   Practice personal reflection and self-correction to assure continual professional development
- EP 2.1.2a   Recognize and manage personal values in a way that allows professional values to guide practice
- EP 2.1.3a   Distinguish, appraise, and integrate multiple sources of knowledge, including research-based knowledge and practice wisdom
- EP 2.1.4   Engage diversity and difference in practice
- EP 2.1.4a   Recognize the extent to which a culture's structures and values may oppress, marginalize, alienate, or create or enhance privilege and power
- EP 2.1.4b   Gain sufficient self-awareness to eliminate the influence of personal biases and values in working with diverse groups
- EP 2.1.4c   Recognize and communicate their understanding of the importance of difference in shaping life experiences
- EP 2.1.5   Advance human rights and social and economic justice
- EP 2.1.5a   Understand forms and mechanisms of oppression and discrimination
- EP 2.1.5b   Advocate for human rights and social and economic justice
- EP 2.1.5c   Engage in practices that advance social and economic justice
- EP 2.1.7b   Critique and apply knowledge to understand person and environment
- EP 2.1.8a   Analyze, formulate, and advocate for policies that advance social well-being
- EP 2.1.9a   Continuously discover, appraise, and attend to changing locales, populations, scientific and technological developments, and emerging societal trends to provide relevant services

A.   **Brief Description**

You will discuss your feelings about serious economic issues involving wealth, poverty, and inequality.

B.   **Objectives**

You will:

1.   Examine your own economic status, the reasons for such status, and your "personal values" about this status.[1]

---

[1] See Council on Social Work Education (CSWE) *Educational Policy and Accreditation Standards (EPAS)* Educational Policy (EP) 2.1.2 ("Apply social work ethical principles to guide professional practice").

2. "Recognize the extent to which a culture's structures and values may oppress, marginalize, alienate, or create or enhance privilege and power" both at the national and global levels.[2]

3. Identify and propose potential means of advocacy "for human rights and social and economic justice."[3]

C.   Procedure

1. Review the content in the text on poverty and economic inequality on the global level.

2. The class will be divided into small groups of four to six.

3. The instructor will ask you to discuss the questions posed below in "D. Instructions for Students" concerning global poverty and economic inequality.

4. The groups will be asked to discuss as instructed below, select a group representative, and be prepared to report to the entire class the small group's findings.

5. After about 15 minutes, the small groups will be asked to terminate their discussions and participate in a full-class discussion.

6. A representative from each group will be asked to share her or his summary of the discussion. Comments will be encouraged from others in the class.

D.   Instructions for Students

After your instructor has divided the class into small groups, discuss in your group your answers to the following questions regarding wealth, poverty, and inequality.

Regarding Personal Economic Factors:
- Where do you stand personally in terms of your overall wealth?
- What factors in your own background contributed to your current financial status and your potential future financial status?
- To what extent do you place importance on your own current and future financial status? Explain.

Regarding Gaps in Wealth in the United States:
- What are the reasons for the widening gap in wealth in the United States?
- To what extent do such gaps in wealth contribute to oppression, on the one hand, and privilege and power on the other? Why and how does this occur?
- Can or should something be done about huge economic gaps between the wealthy and the impoverished? If so, what should be done and why?

Regarding Global Poverty:
- What are the reasons for such extreme global poverty?
- What can or should be done to help?

---

[2] See *EPAS* 2.1.4 ("Engage diversity and difference in practice").
[3] See *EPAS* 2.1.5 ("Advance human rights and social and economic justice").

Focus Competencies or Practice Behaviors:
- EP 2.1.3a   Distinguish, appraise, and integrate multiple sources of knowledge, including research-based knowledge and practice wisdom
- EP 2.1.7   Apply knowledge of human behavior and the social environment
- EP 2.1.7a   Utilize conceptual frameworks to guide the processes of assessment, intervention, and evaluation
- EP 2.1.7b   Critique and apply knowledge to understand person and environment

A.   **Brief Description**
You are asked to match the five conceptual frameworks concerning functions of communities with their respective definitions, and discuss the basic concepts involved.

B.   **Objectives**
You will:
1.   Explore the functions of communities as part of "the range of social systems in which people live."[4]
2.   Identify the primary concepts involved in conceptual frameworks concerning community functions.
3.   "Apply knowledge to understand person and environment" by assessing the similarities and differences among community functions.[5]

C.   **Procedure**
1.   The instructor will provide you with a visual representation of the information presented below.
2.   The instructor will either break the class into small groups for discussion or ask you individually to match community function with the appropriate definition.
3.   As a basis for a full-class discussion, the instructor will propose the subsequent questions posed below.

D.   **Instructions for Students**
1.   Match the following theoretical functions of communities with their respective descriptions:

Theoretical Function of Communities (Warren, 1983)
1.   Production-distribution-consumption
2.   Socialization
3.   Social control
4.   Social participation
5.   Mutual support

---

[4] See *EPAS* 2.1.7 ("Apply knowledge of human behavior and the social environment").
[5] See *EPAS* 2.1.7.

_____ A.   Concerns the involvement of citizens in social, political, and economic processes.

_____ B.   Relates to "local participation in the process of producing, distributing, and consuming those goods and services that are a part of daily living and access to which is desirable in the immediate locality" (pp. 28-29).

_____ C.   Involves encouragement, assistance, caring, and cooperation among people in communities.

_____ D.   Involves "the process through which a group influences the behavior of its members toward conformity with its norms" (p. 29).

_____ E.   Concerns a "process by which society or one of its constituent social units transmits prevailing knowledge, social values, and behavior patterns to its members" (p. 29).

2.   After matching, answer and respond to the following:
   a.   What concepts in the definitions characterize each function and make that function unique?
   b.   What are the similarities and differences among the functions?

Competencies/Practice Behaviors Exercise 13.3
How Does Your Community Function?

Focus Competencies or Practice Behaviors:
- EP 2.1.1b   Practice personal reflection and self-correction to assure continual professional development
- EP 2.1.3a   Distinguish, appraise, and integrate multiple sources of knowledge, including research-based knowledge and practice wisdom
- EP 2.1.7   Apply knowledge of human behavior and the social environment
- EP 2.1.7a   Utilize conceptual frameworks to guide the processes of assessment, intervention, and evaluation
- EP 2.1.7b   Critique and apply knowledge to understand person and environment

A.   **Brief Description**
   You are asked to discuss how the five theoretical functions of communities apply to your own home communities.

B.   Objectives
You will:
1.   Examine five conceptual frameworks concerning functions characterizing communities in order to better understand communities as part "of the range of social systems in which people live."[6]
2.   "Apply knowledge to understand person and environment" by appraising how your own home communities fulfill these functions.[7]

C.   Procedure
1.   Review content on the five theoretical functions of communities.
2.   The class will break into small groups of five or six.
3.   Address the questions posed below.
4.   Each group should select a representative to report the group's findings to the class.
5.   After 10 to 15 minutes, the groups will be asked to share their findings for a full-class discussion.

D.   Instructions for Students
After your instructor divides the class into small groups, address the following questions:
1.   How does the community in which you live fulfill the five theoretical functions characterizing communities? They are:
    a.   Production-distribution-consumption
    b.   Socialization
    c.   Social control
    d.   Social participation
    e.   Mutual support
2.   If something is lacking, how might community functioning be improved?

Competencies/Practice Behaviors Exercise 13.4
Assessing Feminist Principles on a Global Basis

Focus Competencies or Practice Behaviors:
- EP 2.1.1b   Practice personal reflection and self-correction to assure continual
- EP 2.1.2a   Recognize and manage personal values in a way that allows professional values to guide practice
- EP 2.1.3a   Distinguish, appraise, and integrate multiple sources of knowledge, including research-based knowledge and practice wisdom
- EP 2.1.4   Engage diversity and difference in practice
- EP 2.1.4a   Recognize the extent to which a culture's structures and values may oppress, marginalize, alienate, or create or enhance privilege and power

---

[6] See *EPAS* 2.1.7.
[7] See *EPAS* 2.1.7.

- EP 2.1.4b   Gain sufficient self-awareness to eliminate the influence of personal biases and values in working with diverse groups
- EP 2.1.4c   Recognize and communicate their understanding of the importance of difference in shaping life experiences
- EP 2.1.5   Advance human rights and social and economic justice
- EP 2.1.5a   Understand forms and mechanisms of oppression and discrimination
- EP 2.1.5b   Advocate for human rights and social and economic justice
- EP 2.1.5c   Engage in practices that advance social and economic justice
- EP 2.1.7   Apply knowledge of human behavior and the social environment
- EP 2.1.7a   Utilize conceptual frameworks to guide the processes of assessment, intervention, and evaluation
- EP 2.1.7b   Critique and apply knowledge to understand person and environment
- EP 2.1.8a   Analyze, formulate, and advocate for policies that advance social well-being
- EP 2.1.8b   Collaborate with colleagues and clients for effective policy action
- EP 2.1.9a   Continuously discover, appraise, and attend to changing locales, populations, scientific and technological developments, and emerging societal trends to provide relevant services

A.   Brief Description

You will address case examples of feminist principles as applied to global development.

B.   Objectives

You will:

1.   "Utilize [feminist] conceptual frameworks to guide the process… of assessment" while examining case examples of global social development.[8]
2.   Recognize your own values concerning, beliefs in, and commitment to such feminist principles.[9]
3.   Explore the usefulness of feminist principles to "advance social and economic justice."[10]

C.   Procedure

1.   Review the content in the text on community development practice and social development.
2.   The instructor will provide a handout of the principles and their respective case examples presented below (taken directly from Highlight 13.3 in the text).
3.   After reading or summarizing the handout, the instructor will present the class with the subsequent questions presented below for a full-class discussion.

D.   Instructions for Students

1.   Your instructor will read or describe the following content identifying four feminist principles and their application to cases involving global development.

---

[8] See *EPAS* 2.1.7.
[9] See *EPAS* 2.1.2.
[10] See *EPAS* 2.1.5.

Highlight 13.4: A Feminist Perspective on Global Development

Community development can emphasize improving the status of and conditions for women. Ferree (2010) suggests that focusing on gender can serve at least three purposes. First, women can be encouraged to participate in political activities on their own behalf. Second, such a gender-oriented perspective can "empower women to challenge limitations on their roles and lives" (p. 294). Third, a focus on gender can "create networks among women that enhance their ability to recognize existing gender relations as oppressive and in need of change" (pp. 294-295). Such perspectives can boost confidence and, in turn, result in an increased sense of self-worth.

Wetzel (1995) discusses the importance of women's mental health on a global level as a necessity to maintain their optimal well-being. She cites several standards based on feminist principles that should govern the development of programs for women around the world. For each she provides an international example. Although programs may vary, they should address the improvement of women's self-concepts, increasing their ability to act assertively on their own behalves, and enhance supportive relationships.

Standard 1. "Raising consciousness regarding gender roles and the importance and worth of every female" (p. 181). Work that is traditionally "women's work" should be respected and appreciated as work just as traditional "men's work" is outside of the home. The rights and emotional well-being of women deserve respect.

Filomena Tomaira Pacsi, a women's social action group in Peru, provides an example. The issue addressed the plight of the wives of rural miners who were traditionally belittled and abused by their spouses. *Filomena* consisted of a group of urban women from Lima who worked with these rural women "to reduce their feeling of isolation (negative aloneness), enhance their solidarity (positive connectedness), encourage social action, and increase their self-perception and sense of worth by recognizing how important their roles are to their husbands, children, and communities. ... The urban women of *Filomena* joined with these rural women to raise their consciousness and change their lives. When the mines were being closed without notice, the rural women encouraged their husbands and families to make sacrifice marches hundreds of miles to the city. With the help of *Filomena,* the women of Lima began to realize how important they were to the mining struggle. The rural women took charge of the marches, feeding their families in community kitchens and providing education for their children along the way. The women also took responsibility for health care, surveying the needs of children and arranging for mobile health units staffed by paramedics ... The presence of the urban women of *Filomena,* in the words of the rural women of the mines, brought them 'tremendous joy, sweeping them off their feet.' The solidarity and spirit of the two groups of women spread to the rural women's husbands, who stopped being violent toward their wives and showed them newfound respect. Respect for the rural women's roles was enhanced by bonding among the women and the recognition of their organizational expertise. It was the women who taught their husbands to advocate for better working conditions rather than to settle for their poor circumstances. The women opened their husbands' eyes to the responsibilities of companies and the rights of human beings in their employ" (p. 182).

Standard 2. "Forming interdisciplinary professional partnerships with poor women and training indigenous [those originating in the community] *trainers to serve their own communities"* (p. 182). It's important for professionals from various backgrounds to work together with poor women to train them. These poor women then, in turn, can return to and help their own communities by providing training for the women there.

The Women in Development Consortium of Thailand was a program co-sponsored by three Thai universities in conjunction with York University in Canada. The project called "Train the Trainers" was undertaken by "Friends of Women, an interdisciplinary group of professional women and a few men who [were] … kindred spirits. These women and men [were] … devoted to working in partnership with low-income female factory workers who [were] … exploited. Using a nonhierarchical participative group approach, the professional facilitators train[ed] selected leaders from the factory, who in turn train[ed] the other female factory workers, hence, the Train the Trainer program title."

The training included five parts. First, the participants' feelings of isolation were addressed and their connectedness as a potentially supportive group emphasized. Most participants originated in rural areas and traveled to work in the relatively better economic urban environment. The second part of training involved health concerns in an industrial setting including "chronic exhaustion from devastating working conditions" (p. 182). The third training segment addressed participants' individual economic issues such as "personal incomes and expenses, analyzing their situations in the context of their poor status" (p. 182). "[F]eminist labor lawyers and educators" led the fourth phase where labor laws and rights were discussed. Collective bargaining and lobbying in the political arena were also explained. The fifth training unit concerned a "synthesis" of all that participants had learned. "[C]onnections between personal and social problems and economic and political concerns … [were clearly identified.] The necessity of working individually and collectively for social change" was emphasized. The process resulted in participants' enhanced self-esteem and vision concerning what they might be able to achieve. Participants could then return to their factory environments and share what they learned with other workers.

Standard 3. "Teaching women that both personal development and action, as well as collective social development and action, are essential if their lives are to change for the better" (p. 186). We have identified feminist principles that stress how consciousness raising, an enhanced perception of one's life circumstances, and an increased understanding of self are extremely important for women. We have also emphasized that, according to feminist theories, the personal is political. Personal development is fine, but it must coincide with political and social action. Only then can conditions be improved and social justice be attained for all women.

An example of a program adopting this standard is *Stree Mukti Sanghatana,* a group that uses street theater to raise consciousness and advocate for women's rights in Bombay, India. Dramatic performances, entertainment, and other visual media such as posters serve as conduits to convey information and identify issues. Examples of performances include "*No Dowry, Please; We Will Smash the Prison*; and *A Girl is Born,* all of which address traumatic examples of female subordination" (p. 187).

2.   The class will address the following questions:
    a.   To what extent do you agree with the three feminist principles presented?
    b.   How valuable did the principles seem in implementing the thre programmatic examples? Explain.
    c.   To what extent do these feminist principles help to advance social an economic justice? Explain.

Competencies/Practice Behaviors Exercise 13.5
Cultural Differences in a Global Context and You

Focus Competencies or Practice Behaviors:

- EP 2.1.1b   Practice personal reflection and self-correction to assure continual
- EP 2.1.2a   Recognize and manage personal values in a way that allows professional values to guide practice
- EP 2.1.3a   Distinguish, appraise, and integrate multiple sources of knowledge, including research-based knowledge and practice wisdom
- EP 2.1.4   Engage diversity and difference in practice
- EP 2.1.4a   Recognize the extent to which a culture's structures and values may oppress, marginalize, alienate, or create or enhance privilege and power
- EP 2.1.4b   Gain sufficient self-awareness to eliminate the influence of personal biases and values in working with diverse groups
- EP 2.1.4c   Recognize and communicate their understanding of the importance of difference in shaping life experiences
- EP 2.1.5   Advance human rights and social and economic justice
- EP 2.1.5a   Understand forms and mechanisms of oppression and discrimination
- EP 2.1.7b   Critique and apply knowledge to understand person and environment
- EP 2.1.9a   Continuously discover, appraise, and attend to changing locales, populations, scientific and technological developments, and emerging societal trends to provide relevant services

A.   **Brief Description**
You will address cultural differences in a global context.

B.   Objectives

You will:

1.   Examine four cultural differences characterizing various parts of the globe.
2.   "Recognize and communicate your understanding of the importance of difference in shaping life experiences" at the global level.[11]
3.   Assess your values concerning these differences in preparation for managing these personal values and allowing "professional values to guide practice."[12]

C.   Procedure

1.   Review the content in the text on social work values and cross-cultural values from a global perspective.
2.   The instructor will provide a handout to students of the principles and their respective case examples presented below (taken directly from Highlight 13.7 in the text).
3.   After reading or summarizing the handout, the instructor will present the class with the subsequent questions presented below for a full-class discussion.

D.   Instructions for Students

1.   Your instructor will read or describe the following content identifying four cultural differences apparent around the globe.

Highlight 13.7: Cultural Differences in an Organizational Context

Dubrin (2007, pp. 386-387) cites four cultural differences in the context of working with and in organizations (Hofstede, 1980, 1993; Kennedy & Everest, 1991). These also are significant when working effectively with organizations in the community environment and with community citizens. It's essential to establish goals with community residents that fit well with their own value systems. It's also crucial for people commencing community development to be aware of their own value orientations so as not to impose them on people in the community.

1.   *Individualism versus collectivism. Individualism* is "a mental set in which people see themselves first as individuals and believe that their own interests take priority. At the other end of the continuum, *collectivism* is a feeling that the group and society receive top priority. … Highly individualistic cultures include the United States, Canada, Great Britain, Australia, and the Netherlands. Japan, Taiwan, Mexico, Greece, and Hong Kong are among the countries that strongly value collectivism" (Dubrin, 2007, p. 386).

Sowers and Rowe (2007) comment concerning differences in how individual importance is perceived:

---

[11] See *EPAS* 2.1.4.
[12] See *EPAS* 2.1.2.

"For instance, within the African context, traditional African thinking understands human nature and human flourishing as a network of life forces that emanate from God and end in God, who is the source of all life forces. For many Africans, personhood is attainable only in community and the single most important concept within African traditional life is the inclusion of all into the community (Senghor, 1966; Setiloane, 1986)" (p. 30).

Van Wormer (2006) reflects on the value of collectivism for First Nations Peoples:

> "The sense of interconnectedness is a staple of traditional indigenous culture. The First Nations people in North American rely on the metaphor of the Medicine Wheel, which exemplifies the wholeness of all life. The Medicine Wheel teaches about the cycle of life, a cycle that encompasses infancy through old age, the seasons, and four directions of human growth—the emotional, mental, physical, and spiritual. This is not a linear system; all the parts are interconnected. American Indian teachings are traditionally presented as narratives and shared within a talking circle. … [V]alues are: a strong emphasis on *being* not doing and cooperation over competition; a group emphasis; working only to meet one's needs; nonmaterialism; … and living in harmony with nature.
>
> The theme of these values is social interconnectedness" (p. 57).

Sowers and Rowe (2007) conclude that "working out an understanding of human beings and personal development that incorporates cultural conceptions and beliefs is critical to effective social work practice, particularly in a global context" (p. 30).

2. *Materialism versus concern for others. Materialism* is the value that material things and money are extremely important, much more so than humanitarian or spiritual pursuits. There is also a tendency to emphasize, "Me Me Me," rather than focus on other people's needs and issues. In contrast, *concern for others* refers to genuine, active concern for other people's well-being and a focus on the importance of interpersonal relationships. "Materialistic countries include Japan, Austria, and Italy. The United States is considered to be moderately materialistic … Scandinavian nations all emphasize caring as a national value" (Dubrin, 2007, p. 386).

3. *Formality versus informality.* "A country that values *formality* attaches considerable importance to tradition, ceremony, social rules, and rank. At the other extreme, *informality* refers to a casual attitude toward tradition, ceremony, social rules, and rank. … [People] in Latin American countries highly value formality, such as lavish public receptions and processions. Americans, Canadians, and Scandinavians are much more informal" (Dubrin, 2007, p. 386).

4. *Urgent time orientation versus casual time orientation.* "Individuals and nations attach different importance to time. People with an *urgent time orientation* perceive time as a scarce resource and tend to be impatient. People with a *casual time orientation* view time as an unlimited and unending resource and tend to be patient. Americans are noted for their urgent time orientation. They frequently impose deadlines and are eager to get started doing business. Asians and Middle Easterners, in contrast are [much more] patient" (Dubrin, 2007, p. 387).

2. You will address the following questions:
   - How would you describe yourself concerning these four value dimensions and why?
   - To what extent do you think you would find it difficult to work with people holding different views and values than your own.
   - What might you do to improve your ability to accept and appreciate the values of others, and work effectively with clients who hold values differing from your own?

REFERENCES

Council on Social Work Education (CSWE). (2008). *Educational policy and accreditation standards (EPAS).* Alexandria, VA: Author. (Available at www.cswe.org.)

Dubrin, A. (2007). *Fundamentals of organizational behavior* (4th ed.). Mason, OH: South-Western.

Ferree, M. M. (2012). Globalization and feminism: Opportunities and obstacles for activism in the global arena. In D. S. Eitzen & M. B. Zinn (Eds.), *Globalization: The transformation of social worlds* (3rd ed., pp. 291-302). Belmont, CA: Wadsworth.

Hofstede, G. (1980). *Culture's consequences: International differences in work-related values.* Thousand Oaks, CA: Sage.

Hofstede, G. (1993, Spring). A conversation with Geert Hofstede. *Organizational Dynamics,* 50-54.

Kennedy, J., & Everest, A. (1991, September). Put diversity in context. *Personnel Journal,* 50-54.

Senghor, L. S. (1966). Negritude. *Optima, 16,* 1-8.

Setiloane, G. M. (1986). *African theology: An introduction.* Johannesburg: Skotaville.

Sowers, K. M., & Rowe, W. S. (2007). *Social work practice & social justice: From local to global perspectives.* Belmont, CA: Brooks/Cole.

van Wormer, K. (2006). *Introduction to social welfare and social work: The U.S. in global perspective.* Belmont, CA: Brooks/Cole.

Warren, R. (1983). A community model. In R. M. Kramer & H. Specht (Eds.), *Readings in community organization practice* (pp. 28-36). Englewood Cliffs, NJ: Prentice-Hall.

Wetzel, J. W. (1995). Global feminist zeitgeist practice. In N. Van Den Bergh (ED.), *Feminist practice in the 21st century* (pp. 175-192). Washington, DC: NASW Press.

Chapter 13 Competencies/Practice Behaviors Exercises Assessment:

Name: _____ **Date:** _____

Supervisor's Name: _____

Focus Competencies/Practice Behaviors:

- EP 2.1.1b   Practice personal reflection and self-correction to assure continual professional development
- EP 2.1.2a   Recognize and manage personal values in a way that allows professional values to guide practice
- EP 2.1.3a   Distinguish, appraise, and integrate multiple sources of knowledge, including research-based knowledge and practice wisdom
- EP 2.1.4   Engage diversity and difference in practice
- EP 2.1.4a   Recognize the extent to which a culture's structures and values may oppress, marginalize, alienate, or create or enhance privilege and power
- EP 2.1.4b   Gain sufficient self-awareness to eliminate the influence of personal biases and values in working with diverse groups
- EP 2.1.4c   Recognize and communicate their understanding of the importance of difference in shaping life experiences
- EP 2.1.5   Advance human rights and social and economic justice
- EP 2.1.5a   Understand forms and mechanisms of oppression and discrimination
- EP 2.1.5b   Advocate for human rights and social and economic justice
- EP 2.1.5c   Engage in practices that advance social and economic justice
- EP 2.1.7   Apply knowledge of human behavior and the social environment
- EP 2.1.7a   Utilize conceptual frameworks to guide the processes of assessment, intervention, and evaluation
- EP 2.1.7b   Critique and apply knowledge to understand person and environment
- EP 2.1.8a   Analyze, formulate, and advocate for policies that advance social well-being
- EP 2.1.8b   Collaborate with colleagues and clients for effective policy action
- EP 2.1.9a   Continuously discover, appraise, and attend to changing locales, populations, scientific and technological developments, and emerging societal trends to provide relevant services

Instructions:

A.   Evaluate your work or your partner's work in the Focus Competencies/Practice Behaviors by completing the Competencies/Practice Behaviors Assessment form below

B.   What other Competencies/Practice Behaviors did you use to complete these Exercises? Be sure to record them in your assessments

1.	I have attained this competency/practice behavior (in the range of 81 to 100%)						
2.	I have largely attained this competency/practice behavior (in the range of 61 to 80%)						
3.	I have partially attained this competency/practice behavior (in the range of 41 to 60%)						
4.	I have made a little progress in attaining this competency/practice behavior (in the range of 21 to 40%)						
5.	I have made almost no progress in attaining this competency/practice behavior (in the range of 0 to 20%)						

EPAS 2008 Core Competencies & Core Practice Behaviors	Student Self Assessment						Evaluator Feedback
Student and Evaluator Assessment Scale and Comments	0	1	2	3	4	5	Agree/Disagree /Comments
EP 2.1.1 Identify as a Professional Social Worker and Conduct Oneself Accordingly:							
a. Advocate for client access to the services of social work							
b. Practice personal reflection and self-correction to assure continual professional development							
c. Attend to professional roles and boundaries							
d. Demonstrate professional demeanor in behavior, appearance, and communication							
e. Engage in career-long learning							
f. Use supervision and consultation							
EP 2.1.2 Apply Social Work Ethical Principles to Guide Professional Practice:							
a. Recognize and manage personal values in a way that allows professional values to guide practice							
b. Make ethical decisions by applying NASW Code of Ethics and, as applicable, of the IFSW/IASSW Ethics in Social Work, Statement of Principles							
c. Tolerate ambiguity in resolving ethical conflicts							
d. Apply strategies of ethical reasoning to arrive at principled decisions							
EP 2.1.3 Apply Critical Thinking to Inform and Communicate Professional Judgments:							
a. Distinguish, appraise, and integrate multiple sources of knowledge, including research-based knowledge and practice wisdom							
b. Analyze models of assessment, prevention, intervention, and evaluation							
c. Demonstrate effective oral and written communication in working with individuals, families, groups, organizations, communities, and colleagues							
EP 2.1.4 Engage Diversity and Difference in Practice:							
a. Recognize the extent to which a culture's structures and values may oppress, marginalize, alienate, or create or enhance privilege and power							
b. Gain sufficient self-awareness to eliminate the influence of personal biases and values in working with diverse groups							
c. Recognize and communicate their understanding of the importance of difference in shaping life experiences							
d. View themselves as learners and engage those with whom they work as informants							

EP 2.1.5 Advance Human Rights and Social and Economic Justice:							
a. Understand forms and mechanisms of oppression and discrimination							
b. Advocate for human rights and social and economic justice							
c. Engage in practices that advance social and economic justice							
EP 2.1.6 Engage in Research-Informed Practice and Practice-Informed Research:							
a. Use practice experience to inform scientific inquiry							
b. Use research evidence to inform practice							
EP 2.1.7 Apply Knowledge of Human Behavior and the Social Environment:							
a. Utilize conceptual frameworks to guide the processes of assessment, intervention, and evaluation							
b. Critique and apply knowledge to understand person and environment							
EP 2.1.8 Engage in Policy Practice to Advance Social and Economic Well-Being and to Deliver Effective Social Work Services:							
a. Analyze, formulate, and advocate for policies that advance social well-being							
b. Collaborate with colleagues and clients for effective policy action							
EP 2.1.9 Respond to Contexts that Shape Practice:							
a. Continuously discover, appraise, and attend to changing locales, populations, scientific and technological developments, and emerging societal trends to provide relevant services							
b. Provide leadership in promoting sustainable changes in service delivery and practice to improve the quality of social services							
EP 2.1.10 Engage, Assess, Intervene, and Evaluate with Individuals, Families, Groups, Organizations and Communities:							
a. Substantively and affectively prepare for action with individuals, families, groups, organizations, and communities							
b. Use empathy and other interpersonal skills							
c. Develop a mutually agreed-on focus of work and desired outcomes							
d. Collect, organize, and interpret client data							
e. Assess client strengths and limitations							
f. Develop mutually agreed-on intervention goals and objectives							
g. Select appropriate intervention strategies							
h. Initiate actions to achieve organizational goals							
i. Implement prevention interventions that enhance client capacities							
j. Help clients resolve problems							
k. Negotiate, mediate, and advocate for clients							
l. Facilitate transitions and endings							
m. Critically analyze, monitor, and evaluate interventions							

CPSIA information can be obtained
at www.ICGtesting.com
Printed in the USA
FFOW05n2226071013
1998FF

9 781285 4